The
DON'T PANIC PANTRY
Cookbook

The

DON'T PANIC PANTRY

Cookbook

MOSTLY VEGETARIAN COMFORT FOOD
THAT HAPPENS TO BE PRETTY GOOD FOR YOU

noah galuten

PHOTOGRAPHS BY KRISTIN TEIG

 ALFRED A. KNOPF · NEW YORK · 2023

THIS IS A BORZOI BOOK
PUBLISHED BY ALFRED A. KNOPF

www.aaknopf.com

Knopf, Borzoi Books, and the colophon are registered
trademarks of Penguin Random House LLC.

Library of Congress Cataloging-in-Publication Data
Names: Galuten, Noah, author. | Teig, Kristin, photographer.
Title: The don't panic pantry cookbook : mostly vegetarian comfort food that happens
    to be pretty good for you / Noah Galuten ; photographs by Kristin Teig.
Description: First edition. | New York : Alfred A. Knopf, 2023. | Includes index.
Identifiers: LCCN 2022002869 | ISBN 9780593319833 (hardcover) |
    ISBN 9780593319840 (ebook)
Subjects: LCSH: Cooking, Italian. | Cooking, American. | Cooking (Vegetables) |
    LCGFT: Cookbooks.
Classification: LCC TX723 .G243 2022 | DDC 641.5—dc23/eng/20220419
LC record available at https://lccn.loc.gov/2022002869

Cover photographs by Kristin Teig
Cover design by Jenny Carrow

Manufactured in China

First Edition

For my wife, Iliza,
my inspiration, the heartbeat of our tiny family, and,
as of quite recently, my second favorite person in the world.

For our daughter, Sierra Mae—
as of quite recently, my favorite person in the world.

CONTENTS

FOREWORD

iliza shlesinger

I mean, of course. Of *course* I am going to say this book is wonderful and so is my husband. It would be great if everyone loved this cookbook and we sold a billion copies. I want everyone to know Noah's delicious recipes and see how talented he is.

But, to be honest? I don't love food, not the way Noah does. I've never taken a real interest in cooking or getting up at 6:00 a.m. to go to a farmers market for lettuces, and I had never even thought about pluralizing "lettuces" before I met Noah.

And, if I'm being honest, it wasn't until we made *Don't Panic Pantry* (our livestream cooking show) that I got a true sense of Noah's passion for food. Prior to the pandemic, Noah cooked and I ate. It was awesome and I respected what he did, but Noah had his passions and his career and I had mine.

Then the pandemic hit. At the start, everyone felt so helpless, and I said to Noah, "Let's do a cooking show. I can entertain people and you can teach people how to cook. It will be something to do." We wanted to do our part with the resources we had. I had an audience and Noah had culinary skills. Together we created a mini world where people could come every day and cook along with us. Well, *with* Noah, while I talked. Every recipe he wrote, everything he made, was simple and comforting. We were trying to encourage people to stay home more and not run to the grocery store every day. The whole idea behind *Don't Panic Pantry* was "don't panic, you can use alternative ingredients. Don't panic, you can use what you have. Don't panic, we are here to entertain you. Don't panic, you can be of one culture and cook from another. Don't panic, you aren't alone and you can hang out with us in our kitchen for about a half hour every day. We are going to get through this together." Our show, like Noah's food, started out with the purest of intentions—to share information about cooking and make people feel good. And this cookbook is an extension of that show and of Noah. This book is a deeper look at his culinary world. It's a peek into how and why he cooks how he does.

When people find out my husband is a chef, they always ask, "Does he cook for you?" I always say yes, but the real answer is that he doesn't cook as much as he creates. He creates recipes and he really takes time to understand what he is making. There's thought and love behind his dishes that's all so impressive to me. Whether he's seeking out education on the cultural history of a dish, the origin of his produce, or putting a thoughtful twist on someone else's recipe, Noah's food has integrity—it has heart. These recipes aren't intimidating; there's nothing overreaching. That's what I love the most about this book. Noah makes cooking accessible without compromising on what he is doing.

I'm proud of the show we created. I'm proud that he committed to cooking and sharing recipes for our audience for more than 230 episodes. I'm so proud he was able to turn the show into this gorgeous, heartfelt, and informative cookbook. Most important of all, I'm proud to be his wife and eat his food.

INTRODUCTION

"What am I supposed to eat?"

As the world changes around us, we are negotiating constantly with two different versions of ourselves: the one who wants to be healthier and the one who wants to be excited, or comforted, by the food that we eat. Our reflective selves are at odds with our impulsive selves—we eat impulsively and then we diet impulsively. We toggle between extremes, never feeling great about either decision.

The truth is that food is very personal. It is tangled and mixed up with how we feel about our bodies, our pleasure, our shame, our feelings of social responsibility, our relationships with our mothers—everything. Trying to figure out what to eat is, frankly, overwhelming. We all want to eat "better," in every sense of the word. But what does that mean? How do you do The Right Thing when there are ten different versions of The Right Thing—and they are often in direct opposition to one another?

When we try to face these questions on our own, the answers are endlessly confusing. The Internet only seems to offer solutions in the form of self-promotion or righteous indignation. Personal trainers tell you to eat the boneless, skinless breasts of horribly treated chickens, portioned out like dystopian protein cubes; vegan solutions can arrive in the form of chorizo-flavored soybeans piled onto fried corn chips with cashew cream; ketogenic dieters tell you to eat canned sardines for lunch at your desk and mozzarella balls for breakfast—all of them promising that this will somehow lead to a better life.

So where is the rational middle ground? What does "good for you" even mean? How do you worry about your diet, your body, the planet, your happiness, and your schedule all at the same time? What if you like the idea of being a vegetarian but also want to eat meat sometimes?

This book is here to tell you:

Don't Panic.

Don't panic about learning how to cook. Don't panic about environmental sustainability. Don't panic about nutrition. I want you to know that trying matters; that perfection does not exist and that *better* is enough. I believe that extremes are not the answer and that the truth, as always, lies in the gray area.

Enter: *The Don't Panic Pantry Cookbook*. In this Too-Much-Information Age, I have simplified my home cooking philosophy into a few key, pragmatic points:

1. Too much of any one thing is bad.
2. Balance is good.
3. Refined sugar is bad (and it is hiding *everywhere*).

4. Heavily processed food is bad (this is where the sugar is hiding).
5. We should be eating less meat, and higher quality meat.
6. Everyone is focused on protein when they should be focused on fiber.
7. Stock your pantry to make home cooking the *more convenient* option.

These aren't rules, but goals. *Don't Panic Pantry* is not here to teach you how to cheat your diet or trick your body. It is here to show you how to balance it without compromising on quality or thoughtfulness. I want you to know how to make a vegetable rice bowl and an aggressively healthful smoothie—but to also be able to make pasta and tomato sauce at the last minute for six people who you did not realize were suddenly staying for dinner. Don't panic. There's no need.

When the pandemic hit, my wonderful wife, Iliza—who also happens to be an immensely successful stand-up comedian—had to suspend her worldwide comedy tour. All of a sudden, just like everyone else, we were stuck at home. Everyone was panic-buying rice and beans and lentils and frozen vegetables, and so many people

were suddenly realizing that they had no idea what to do with it all. So Iliza and I thought that it would be a good idea to do a live-stream cooking show as a way to connect with her fans and take advantage of having a chef and cookbook author (me) for a husband. We started off with one of my favorite childhood recipes, Pasta Fazool (page 109)—an easy, quick, nutritious dinner involving canned tomatoes, canned white beans, dried pasta, and whatever fresh or frozen greens you have on hand. I posted a (very loose) recipe in advance and the two of us just stood in our home kitchen, cooking, cracking jokes, and answering questions from the comment section.

The response we got was immense. People were desperate for recipes and human connection, but also for a voice to talk to in the empty void. So the show continued on and we became a meeting place where we encouraged people to limit trips to the grocery store, to cook with what they have, to stay home and to flatten the curve. (Remember that?) For the first 120 episodes, we posted weekly shopping lists and filmed live episodes from Monday through Sunday—for around four months. The show continued long after those first four months, eventually dropping down to twice a week. As the pandemic raged on, we reached out directly to companies that we genuinely liked and formed partnerships. Sometimes we would cook my childhood favorites like a Fillet of Sole (page 159) or Mom's Brown Rice Pudding (38); and sometimes I just experimented with something I had never made before, because I wanted to eat it for dinner that night. It became, frankly, a distraction for me, too—a way to focus on something other than the anxiety that we all felt.

But out of this collective, worldwide trauma came a personal highlight: this cookbook. It is the cookbook I have always wanted to write (deeply personal, filled with pasta and lentils and beans), but informed by hundreds of episodes spent messaging directly with home cooks at every level of experience. It allowed me to teach people to start small.

My first piece of advice is perhaps an obvious one: Learn how to make food that you are willing to eat. That's it. Start there. Then expand. If you are not happy with how it turned out? Don't panic. Just do it again—it will come out better. Then do it a third time. Then try another dish. Learn a few simple building blocks that teach you the basics and then go from there. Pretty soon you'll have something in your back pocket that's easier, faster, cheaper, and better than the mediocre take-out place down the street that you don't really like but keep ordering from anyway.

This cookbook is filled with the food of my childhood, the things I learned from friends and family along the way, and my own personal creations that I've developed over the course of my career as an obsessive home cook, writer, and chef. But it also offers you options. For example, there are two versions of tomato sauce in the book (the one I cook for myself, and the one I cook for company). I have three versions of broccoli pasta in the book: vegetarian (page 100), with homemade pork sausage (page 102), or with anchovies (page 103). I want you to be able to use canned beans, but I also want to show you how to cook a Pot of Beans (page 2) and then utilize them throughout the week in a variety of different recipes. I want you to be able to make a Roasted Sweet Potato (page 59) or learn how to make A Perfect Egg (page 12), cooked to the exact doneness that you like.

But as you can probably assume from the title, the pantry is a big part of this book, too. It is there to set you up for *convenient* success. I grew up with a pantry full of canned tomatoes and garlic and pasta and olive oil—but as I got older and explored my diverse, beautiful hometown of Los Angeles, it also began to fill with ingredients like rice noodles, dried seaweed, chiles de árbol, soy sauce, tamari, sesame oil, turmeric, cumin seeds, black mustard seeds, and anchovies. As I expanded my ideas and learned from more and more people, those bottles and jars and cans began to spill into one another inside of pans and bowls. Now it's hard for me to imagine a world in which olive oil, lemon juice, and tamari are not a perfect trinity. When I learned to make Ghee (page 18)—an Indian technique of clarifying butter—in order to make Shantam's Kitchari (page 36), it made all kinds of sense to use it to make popcorn on the stove, which eventually led to Iliza's favorite version: Shichimi Popcorn (page 46). Growing up in Southern California and going to health food stores with my dad meant that tamari was a huge part of my childhood, and that rosemary was growing everywhere. Those two ingredients seem like they should always have been together, and do so in a nutritious, healthful snack like the highly addictive Rosemary-Tamari Almonds (page 42).

There is also a simple ingredient like sauerkraut. (I know it seems like it only belongs in German food, but I promise it's just cabbage and salt that has been squished together and allowed to ferment.) It adds a sour, crunchy, healthful, and probiotic burst to dishes like Krauty Beans (page 138)—a staple of the show and our home, making for one of the fastest, tastiest, and most nutritious dishes in the book. But sauerkraut also shows up in a Krauty Smoked Cheddar Broccoli Bread (page 67) that is the vegetarian German-Italian stromboli you never knew belonged in your life.

As I wrote this book, it was also really important to me that the work you do to stock your pantry means that almost all of the ingredients that you use, or staples that you prepare, show up throughout the book. If you are buying turmeric to make Golden Milk (page 33), you will be happy to know that it won't just be left alone forever in your pantry, because it will also be present in Health Sludge (page 32), Shantam's Kitchari (page 36), and the Turmeric Tomato Salad with Fried Herbs and Kitchari Spices (page 88). Along those lines, it was equally important to me, while I encourage shopping at local farmers markets, that almost every ingredient in this book be found at your local grocery store, or ordered online with relative simplicity.

This is not a diet book (though refined sugar barely exists in this book, and only when absolutely necessary). This is not a book about ethical eating. This is comfort food that happens to be pretty good for you and pretty good for the planet. This is the rational middle ground. It is a "Chef Salad" with Cheddar Croutons and Probiotic Ranch (page 87). It is Pasta with Rosemary-Bacon Tomato Sauce (page 104), or a vegetarian version using dried mushrooms instead. It's a thirty-second Vegan Tahini Dressing that you will be tossing with your Hippie California salad (page 81), dipping cucumbers into for crudités, using to dress your Purple Tahini Slaw (page 58), *and* tossing with your Cold Sesame Soba (page 119). It's a Sheet-Pan Miso Roast Chicken with Vegetables (page 169) that you can prep in advance and leave in the fridge for several hours, or even a day before, and then just put in the oven to make a one-pan dinner for your family. But it's also—for when you really need it—the fresh herbed panko crusted Mozzarella Marinara (page 157) that made my wife break down in tears of joy during an episode of *Don't Panic Pantry*.

Marcella and Camus

It all started with slicing garlic cloves and then sautéing them in olive oil. That was (okay, maybe still is) the base of almost all of my cooking. It started with garlic and olive oil. It started with my mom.

I learned to cook from her, and she in turn learned from her mother. Back in the '70s, my parents were borderline hippies, who met when my mom was waiting tables at a vegetarian restaurant in Miami called Here Comes the Sun. They got divorced not long after they moved to California, when I was around two years old. So I grew up eating '80s vegetarian food with my dad from health food stores in Topanga, California: veggie dogs with runny, off-brand ketchup; tofu scramble breakfast burritos; alfalfa sprouts on everything. Meanwhile, my mom's house was a place of hybridization—she would take the Italian-American food that she grew up with and give it a hippie, California twist, often using ground turkey in place of ground beef, or swapping brown rice in for white. My cooking is a direct result of that, and to be perfectly honest, a not-insignificant number of the recipes in this book come directly from my mother. (Her Turkey Pasta [page 97], Broccoli-Sausage Bread [page 64], and Vegan Cal-Italian Black-Eyed Peas [page 71] still get cooked regularly in my home.)

Here's the thing: Some people grow up thinking that Hollywood is an unattainable dream, some far-off impossible thing that is only available to the chosen few. But I grew up in Santa Monica, California. To me, the world of movies and television was just a local industry—a place where my friends' parents worked as screenwriters, or camera operators, or editors, or script supervisors. It was a feasible career path that would in all likelihood be filled with inconsistent employment and long hours.

But someone like, say, Lidia Bastianich? She was special—a chef with a cooking show on *PBS;* a cook who knew how to clean calamari and deep-fry artichokes; a writer who wrote cookbooks and opened restaurants. Lidia and Ming Tsai and Wolfgang Puck were my superheroes. Names like Edna Lewis, Marcella Hazan, and Marion Cunningham sat on the bookshelves of our apartment, carrying equal weight in my head with Vonnegut, Camus, and Lady Murasaki.

Okay fine, I was a weird kid.

But this is all to say that I thought about cookbook authors the way that a starry-eyed ingénue in Kansas thinks about movie stars. It never even occurred to me that a chef or a cookbook author was something that a person could become—you either were one or you were not, and that was that. I *loved* food. I read cookbooks, I

watched food TV. I cooked almost every day. I was the guy in college making Pasta Fazool for all of his friends (did I mention that I was a weird kid?), or who went on ski trips as an excuse to stay back in the cabin and simmer a giant pot of meat sauce because I didn't want to waste money renting skis.

After college, I found myself writing for local newspapers, food blogs, and magazines while waiting tables and bartending in Los Angeles. One of these restaurants was a popular burger and craft beer café called The Golden State (it is no longer there), where I met my friend and future business partner James Starr. We would spend long days talking about ideas for restaurants. One day we realized that there was a BBQ stand in Compton, California, called Bludso's BBQ that made the best BBQ I had ever eaten in my life. Through a series of bizarre events (for the full story, pick up a copy of *The Bludso's BBQ Cookbook*), I started training in Compton with Kevin Bludso at four o'clock in the morning before he eventually talked me into a job as the opening chef of Bludso's Bar & Que—a 130-seat BBQ restaurant and full bar in L.A. From there I gradually evolved into something of a culinary director for our growing company, but truthfully, I was just a conduit. I was an academic putting in a lot of hours in the field. When we wanted to come up with a breakfast burrito for our new coffee shop, Cofax, I ate every great breakfast burrito in Los Angeles until I figured out what ours should be (it involves pit-smoked potatoes and tomatillos). Then I got to train with the brilliant pizzaiolo Frank Pinello of Best Pizza in Williamsburg, Brooklyn, to help us open our New York–style pizzeria, Prime Pizza—which has gone on to have five locations in Los Angeles, and counting.

At the same time, I had the unbelievable good fortune to coauthor my first cookbook—working with a true genius of a chef in Jeremy Fox, for his book *On Vegetables*. Somehow, a guy from Santa Monica who just loved food and writing and cookbooks got to learn from three incredible mentors with completely different backgrounds in Kevin Bludso, Frank Pinello, and Jeremy Fox. Looking back, it feels like I was getting paid to go to some food nerd fantasy camp. Very much to my surprise, I had gone from a literature and cookbook nerd who made food for his friends to someone who had become a chef, restaurant consultant, cookbook author, and food writer.

During this part of my career, there was something important that I learned: Restaurant cooking is very different from home cooking. They are almost entirely unrelated. They are about as related as writing a book is to reading a book—or as doing a load of laundry is to running a laundromat. A chef is not a cook. A chef is a manager. A chef is focused on profitability, labor cost, food cost, scheduling, consistency, speed, waste, efficiency, recipe development, reproducibility, personality management, personal health, employee safety, lawsuits, customer complaints, and a hundred other things. I know chefs who never cook at home. I know a lot of home cooks whose house I would rather go to for dinner than any chef's.

Restaurants are often filled with panic. I'm here to help you keep your house calm. The older I get, the more peace I find in cooking at home (please do not check with my wife to see if this is true).

My point is: You can cook. It is easier than you think and has the capacity to become something that is both deeply rewarding and endlessly fascinating. If you're unsure where to start, just flip through these pages, find a dish that sounds good to you, then give it a try. That's it. Read the recipe. Buy the ingredients. Stock your pantry. Don't panic.

More About Those Guidelines

Remember these, from pages xiii–xiv?

1. Too much of any one thing is bad.
2. Balance is good.
3. Refined sugar is bad (and it is hiding *everywhere*).

4. Heavily processed food is bad (this is where the sugar is hiding).
5. We should be eating less meat, and higher quality meat.
6. Everyone is focused on protein when they should be focused on fiber.
7. Stock your pantry to make home cooking the *more convenient* option.

First off, I want you to know that these are actually based on research published in high-quality scientific journals. Most importantly, I'm only writing about a link between food and health if that link has been substantiated by many studies or clinical trials. I relied heavily on meta-analyses, which means they are the analysis of multiple studies to draw conclusions. Those published articles and studies are listed for your reference in the note on sources (see page 181), but for the sake of expressing this information slightly more simply, I'm just going to write a few quick words on each point.

1. TOO MUCH OF ANY ONE THING IS BAD.
2. BALANCE IS GOOD.

These first two are kind of obvious and they go hand in hand. But it is worth mentioning that variety is good and important. Different ingredients have different nutrients, and your body needs many kinds to get the things that it needs to be healthy. It also makes life a lot less boring. If I only ate kale salads every day it would be a pretty miserable life and I also would not be getting enough vitamin D. Do I repeat a lot of ingredients? Absolutely—but I also try to balance them out with other ones as much as possible.

3. REFINED SUGAR IS BAD (AND IT IS HIDING EVERYWHERE).

If you get *really* bored some time, walk down the cereal aisle, read the nutrition facts, and try to find cereal with no added sugar. It is almost impossible (other than, say, a bag of puffed rice that they hide on the bottom shelf). In fact, start reading all of your food labels. Almost everything has added sugar in it. That almond milk you're getting in your latte? It probably has sugar in it (seriously, ask the person behind the counter if you can see the box . . . just be nice about it). It is hiding in yogurt containers, granola bars, oatmeal, protein powders, smoothies, salad dressings, meat marinades—you name it. When people want to make things taste better, they just add sugar to it and hope that you won't check. As a result, in this book, I really tried to remove sugar from all of the recipes, unless absolutely necessary. (In some cases there is honey or maple syrup. In a very few cases there is actual cane sugar, and only if it is necessary, like in a proper cup of Masala Chai, page 35.)

But why is sugar bad? First off, a review in *The Journal of the American Medical Association* put it pretty plainly by concluding that a high-sugar diet significantly increases your chances of dying of cardiovascular disease. Meanwhile, a recent review of sugar and health published in the *Journal of Obesity and Diabetes* found that the average American consumes about four pounds of refined sugar every

twenty days. That level of sugar consumption is two to three times more than what the American Heart Association recommends as healthy. But sugar is not just a risk for heart disease. There is growing evidence linking sugar to certain types of cancer, as well as liver disease; and excessive sugar consumption also causes poor gut health, weight gain, cavities, and insulin resistance (leading to an 83 percent higher risk of developing type 2 diabetes).

This is all to say that yes: Sugar is bad for you, and a lot of sugar is *very* bad for you.

4. HEAVILY PROCESSED FOOD IS BAD (THIS IS WHERE THE SUGAR IS HIDING).

Heavily processed foods now make up 60 percent of the American diet, and it is where they hide the massive quantity of sugar we eat in this country. Studies have shown that the more processed food people eat, the more sugar they eat, and the more artificial colors and preservatives they eat. When you cook your food from unprocessed or minimally processed ingredients, you have more control and understanding over what actually goes into your body. White sugar, for example, provides no nutrients whatsoever. A grape, meanwhile, contains sugar (fructose), but also calcium, iron, potassium, and phosphorus.

Here's the thing: Humans are wired to seek out energy-dense foods like fish, fruits, and nuts. It's how we were meant to stay alive. Meanwhile, scientists in the processed food industry have cracked the code on mimicking energy-dense foods that we are *wired* to want. And guess what? Sitting at a desk all day eating a bag of energy-dense processed food is not actually good for us. That's why this book tries to provide you with the tools to cook yourself real food, using unprocessed or minimally processed ingredients. It's one thing to eat a cookie for fun and to know that it is sugar—but it is something entirely different to eat hidden sugars all day and not be aware of it.

5. WE SHOULD BE EATING LESS MEAT, AND HIGHER QUALITY MEAT.

There are experts far more qualified than I am to tell you about how horrible industrial animal farming is, how bad it is for the planet and for our bodies. But let's set all of that aside for a moment and focus on two other points that don't get enough attention.

First: We need a lot less protein than we think. People are *obsessed* with "getting enough protein." I've got news for you: You're probably fine. We're probably all getting more than enough protein. A recent review of "protein needs" in the NRC Research Press noted that, if we accepted the highest-published estimates for daily protein needs, we would easily meet our protein needs in any reasonable diet. For reference, the average American diet exceeds the USDA's recommended daily allowance by 60 percent. Is protein important? Absolutely. But the truth is, if you are an omnivore, you are in all likelihood getting way, way more than you need through meat, fish, eggs, milk, cheese, nuts, beans, seeds, lentils, fake-meat burgers, soybean products, and powdered protein supplements.

My second point: Higher quality, sustainably raised meat and seafood actually tastes a whole lot better. Is it more expensive? Absolutely. But that is just another good reason to eat less of it. That is why in this book, I encourage you to seek out local farms and farmers markets or sustainable butchers in your area. If you eat less meat and seafood, of a higher quality, you will feel better and it will also taste better. I know that good-quality meat can be hard to find—but I encourage you to do some research on what's available in your area.

6. EVERYONE IS FOCUSED ON PROTEIN WHEN THEY SHOULD BE FOCUSED ON FIBER.

Fiber is really, really important—and I'm not just saying that because I love lentils and beans. Ready for this? A 2019 study published in *The Lancet*, "Carbohydrate Quality and Human Health: A Series of Systematic Reviews and Meta-analyses," reported that increases in fiber in the diet yield striking reductions in what is called "all-cause mortality." In layman's terms—eating more fiber reduces the chances of *things killing you*. Seems pretty good, right? Increased fiber intake reduces risk of coronary heart disease and diabetes, and contributes to a reduction in cancer deaths and incidence; in stroke incidence; and in colorectal, breast, and esophageal cancer. The key takeaway is that most adults consume less than 20 grams of fiber per day, and should be consuming no less than 25 to 29 grams per day. This finding is not the result of one study, or even a dozen studies—this conclusion was based on 243 different studies and clinical trials that collected 135 million person-years of data. To put it simply: Adding more fiber to your diet is probably the most important takeaway from this entire book.

Okay, so how do you get fiber? Well, here's the bad news: All those fiber cereals and fiber bars? Those are often the very same heavily processed foods that have tons of hidden sugars and preservatives. But the good news? There are *lots* of high-fiber foods that you can eat—and a lot of them are in this book and delicious. Lentils and beans (did I mention that I love lentils and beans), raspberries, peas, oats, broccoli, chia seeds—those are all really high in fiber!

7. STOCK YOUR PANTRY TO MAKE HOME COOKING THE *MORE CONVENIENT* OPTION.

A well-stocked pantry is the key to regular home cooking. If you don't have anything in your pantry, you will in all likelihood decide that it's far easier to order delivery, or pick up food, or go to a restaurant than it is to go to the grocery store, come home, cook, and then clean up. But when you stock your pantry with shelf-stable, nutritious ingredients, you can make cooking at home the more convenient option—the one that is faster, cheaper, easier, and way, way better for you.

I keep my food philosophies fairly simple. I want all of the food that I eat to either be something that I'm really excited about eating, or to be something that is really good for me. If it's not exciting *or* good for me—that's a waste of stomach space. In this book, I tried to create as many recipes as I could that actually achieve both. But how do you actually get yourself to follow through? Stock your pantry.

Speaking of . . .

MY PANTRY

I was raised to believe that you should always, under any circumstances, be prepared to cook dinner for six people who arrive at your home unannounced.

But it's not just about being a good host—stocking your pantry is also about setting yourself up to make cooking at home the faster, more convenient, more nutritious option. So I've broken this section down into three categories: Actual Pantry, Within Arm's Reach, and Fridge and Freezer.

Actual Pantry

This is the biggest cabinet that you have, and the one that you organize beautifully when you first move in, only to see it slowly devolve into an eternal chaos cycle where you kind of remember where everything is, unless it is in the back, in which case you throw it away the next time you have to move. But regardless, this is where you keep the dry ingredients that are the building blocks of your meal. Here are the important ones in mine:

Alliums (Garlic, Onions, Shallots, etc.)

Okay, fine, you probably keep these out on the counter and not in the pantry. But they actually prefer to be in a cool, dark place. I try to keep mine under a kitchen towel. These are the ingredients that will help you layer flavor, and are a huge part of the cooking in my home and in this book. They also last a long time, which is great because I never remember if I bought garlic or onions last time and end up buying them again just to be safe.

Canned Whole Peeled Tomatoes

I'm fairly certain that a can of tomatoes has always existed, in every pantry I've ever had, for my entire life. I prefer to use whole peeled tomatoes rather than crushed or diced, as I find that they are generally of higher quality and have less fillers and additives. It's also important to find out what brands you like. Some of them come in a thicker puree, which can be better for sauce. Others come in more of a juice, which I find to be a lot better for soups. Imported tomatoes can get very expensive and I have found some delightful ones grown right here (where I live) in California. If you're lucky enough to be able to buy them in huge #10 cans from a restaurant you helped open, Alta Cucina are great—but Bianco DiNapoli makes an excellent, widely available California tomato, too.

Dried and Canned Beans

I love beans. I really do. While in this book I will always sing the virtues of cooking with dried beans (see A Pot of Beans, page 2)—and particularly the ones grown by Rancho Gordo—I always keep a few cans of cooked beans in the pantry, too. They are a tremendous source of fiber and protein, are delicious, filling, and can add some thickness and heft to a dinner really quickly. When I know I'm going to be home all week, I tend to just cook a pound of beans and keep them in the fridge to use throughout the week. Beans are cheap, too! Even *expensive* beans are only a few dollars a pound, and can feed a lot of people.

Dried Seaweed

There are so many different types of seaweed out there. Nori is a dried sheet, sold in many ways, including in large sheets for sushi, smaller sheets for snacking, or sliced to top things like rice bowls, salads, and soups. But there are two general categories you will find in this book. One is kombu (or konbu), which is often sold as "dashi kombu," and used to make Vegan Dashi (page 9). The other is any dried, edible seaweed that I use for Pantry Seaweed Salad (page 90), Miso Soup (page 127), and Coconut-Wakame Trail Mix (page 43). There are so many varietals of these out there, but the most common one I use is wakame (a classic for the aforementioned Miso Soup). But look out for any of the great blends of dried edible seaweeds online or in stores, sometimes sold as a "seaweed salad mix," which includes beautifully different colors, shapes, and textures.

Lentils

These are often a part of "reset meals" for me, if I've just returned home from a food-heavy work trip. Green, brown, and black lentils are wonderful in salads or as a side dish on their own—but I most often cook red lentils, which have the unique ability to break down and dissolve and thicken into soups, stews, and longer-cooked dishes like the Barely Beef Chili (page 130) and Shantam's Kitchari (page 36). Meanwhile Red Lentil Pomodoro with Spinach and White Beans (page 143) is something I can always lean on as a backup dinner option when I haven't been shopping in a while and desire something nutritious and comforting.

Pasta, Rice Noodles, and Soba

I grew up eating a lot of pasta and, as a result, there is a lot of it in this book. My favorite widely available pasta brand is De Cecco, but I have also been known to splurge on a higher end dried Italian pasta from time to time. I try to keep a decent variety on hand.

A Long: spaghetti or capellini (for Iliza). These are great for Pasta with Shoyu Butter Clam Sauce (page 106) or served with either of the Tomato Sauces (pages 94–96) and perhaps a few Turkey Meatballs (page 166).

A Medium Soup-Friendly Shape: orecchiette, medium shells, or gnocchi (the slug-like pasta shape, not the dumpling). These are ideal for things like Pasta Fazool (page 109), Mom's Minestrone (page 124), or even any of the broccoli pastas (pages 100–103).

A Small Soup Noodle: ditalini, pastina, or stars. These are the ones you want with homemade Chicken Stock (page 5), black pepper, and grated Parmesan when you are home sick (or homesick).

A Medium Short: rigatoni, fusilli, farfalle, rotelle (wagon wheels), bombolotti (short rigatoni). This is more of a standard, everyday pasta shape that will work with everything from the aforementioned broccoli pastas to Turkey Pasta (page 97), Drunken Late-Night Pantry Pasta (page 107), or Pasta with Rosemary-Bacon Tomato Sauce (page 104).

I also keep rice noodles around, which are a gluten-free option that have a wonderful chewiness that holds up well in stir-fries as well as in things like a Rice Noodle Salad with Kale and Edamame (page 120) or Ginger-Cilantro Chicken Noodle Soup (page 134). Sometimes these are labeled as "pad Thai noodles," though that usually refers to the width and length of the noodle. There are lots of different sizes and styles and I enjoy them all in different ways.

In my pantry, soba noodles—which utilize the highly nutritious and nutty flavor of buckwheat—are also essential. These are usually a blend of wheat flour and buckwheat, and are great in salads, often used in soups, and can be found in the Cold Sesame Soba (page 119) right here in this book—or as a substitute noodle for the Rice Noodle Salad.

Rice

There are many types of rice, and they all serve different purposes and needs. But in general, I always try to have:

Brown Rice: for nuttier flavor and extra fiber, to be used with dishes like Mom's Brown Rice Pudding (page 38).

Short-Grain Japanese Rice: for more glutinous, textured rice. I love this for most rice bowls, Vegan Mapo Tofu (page 150), and Veggie Scrap Fried Rice (page 149).

Long-Grain Rice, like Basmati: for a fluffier rice, and dishes like Green Rice and Black Beans (page 148) or Shantam's Kitchari (page 36).

Within Arm's Reach

These are the things I try to keep within grabbing distance, usually on the counter, or in the closest cupboard to the stove. These are the things you suddenly realize that you want while you are sautéing or simmering something and need to find it as quickly as possible: seasonings, spices, oils, dried herbs.

Black Pepper

Once you grind pepper, it slowly begins to lose its flavor and aroma. Find a pepper mill that you like (don't just keep using the disposable ones from the grocery store), keep it on your counter, and grind it fresh when it is called for. For reasons I cannot properly explain, my pepper mill is the object I spend the most time trying to find in my kitchen.

Butter (I promise you can leave it out on the counter)

I use butter less often than I use olive oil, but a little bit of it to finish off some pasta with tomato sauce or to add a particular quality of fat to the base of a pot of Mom's Minestrone (page 124) is irreplaceable. It also pairs perfectly with

---

SHOYU-BUTTER MUSHROOMS

In a pinch, if you have some mushrooms and want them to taste better than you could reasonably expect, simply sauté them in equal parts butter and soy sauce. That's it. That's the recipe. It is perfect. For extra fun, you can even finish it with some chopped scallions and a squeeze of lemon.

soy sauce. I use unsalted butter (better for cooking and baking), keeping it in the refrigerator for storage, but always leaving a stick of it in a butter dish on the counter at room temperature. The USDA says you can only leave butter out for a day or two, but they also say that you should cook eggs until the yolks are hard and burgers until they are well-done. I have found that if you keep your butter in a covered dish, and the temperature of your kitchen is not too hot, butter can be kept on the counter for 2 to 3 weeks.

Dried Herbs, Spices, and Chiles

The most common ones in this book are dried oregano and crushed red pepper—which add a little accent to pastas and beans, usually first toasted briefly in the oil, where they quickly infuse and then can permeate evenly through the whole dish. But other ingredients like turmeric, cumin seeds, dried basil, chili powder, shichimi, and black mustard seeds are incredibly helpful to keep within grabbing distance.

Oils

Different oils have different flavors and functions. In general, you want:

High-Heat Oil: This is for frying and stir-frying—I like peanut, canola, or grapeseed. Canola can also double as a neutral oil if you need one for things like Caesar Salad Crudités (page 86). These also make a nice base for things like Chile Oil (page 17).

Sesame Oil: I actually use this more for dressings and finishing than for cooking. A little drizzle over some Veggie Scrap Fried Rice (page 149) or used in a vinaigrette can be delightfully nutty and roasty. One note—if you don't use sesame oil very often, it is better to keep it in the refrigerator, as it will lose flavor less quickly.

Extra-Virgin Olive Oil: I always have two extra-virgin olive oils in my pantry—an everyday olive oil (try to find a relatively affordable one that tastes good) and another for finishing. Finishing oil is a lot more fragrant and is something that you always want to keep raw (the flavor changes when it's heated). The everyday olive oil is for things like cooking and simple salad dressings. Or to put it more simply: Use the everyday olive oil to sauté garlic and make sauce—then use the finishing oil to drizzle over the finished plate of pasta.

Salt

Yeah, you probably already have salt. You might even have a bunch of tiny flavored ones that someone gave you as a gift once and you don't know which ones are good for what applications. But the truth is, you really only need two:

Kosher Salt: I prefer Diamond Crystal because it does not contain anticaking agents, and has a nice grain that you can pinch with your fingers. This is your workhorse salt, for seasoning water, protein, dressings, and sauces. It is also much harder to oversalt with this than, say, table salt, because it is less dense.

Finishing Salt: A nice flaky, crunchy sea salt is what I usually use—and I use it for salads, toast, a baguette with butter, sprinkling into a bowl of soup, etc.

(Okay, one caveat: For bread and pizza dough, I use fine sea salt, because it disperses more evenly in the dough—and I always measure the salt for my dough by weight.)

Soy Sauce and Tamari

It is actually worth trying different brands to find the one you like (they really all do taste different). While soy sauce and tamari are very similar, tamari is usually gluten-free and has more of a roasted, soybean-forward flavor. You can use them interchangeably, but I specify which ones I prefer in each recipe for this book. These get used in everything from fried rice to salad dressings and even things like Drunken Late-Night Pantry Pasta (page 107).

Fridge and Freezer

I know that this is technically not a pantry, but it can have much the same function, especially with ingredients that will keep for a long time. Over the course of writing this book, I also bought a reach-in freezer and put it in the garage so that I could test out how well different recipes and sauces freeze and reheat—and let me just say that I *love* having a freezer in the garage. It's like having a grocery store at my house that sells all the food I made a while ago—tomato sauce, chicken stock, turkey pasta sauce, Warm Heirloom Summer Fazool (page 111), minestrone soup—you name it.

Frozen Fruits and Vegetables

Having frozen fruits like blueberries on hand will always give you the option to throw some ingredients into a smoothie (or even some oatmeal). I prefer frozen fruit in smoothies rather than fresh, as they are frozen at their peak ripeness, and also keep the smoothie cold.

While I prefer fresh to frozen vegetables, a few options like frozen spinach, kale, edamame, and peas (the best frozen vegetable) give you a backup option when you want to cook, want some nutrition, and haven't had a chance to go shopping for a while.

Miso

Miso is a paste from Japan, involving an ingredient (usually soybeans, though there are *many* versions) that has been fermented with salt and koji (one of the world's great molds). While it is very popular in dishes like Miso Soup (page 127), it also gives deep umami flavors and complexity to recipes like Sheet-Pan Miso Roast Chicken with Vegetables (page 169). There are various styles of miso paste, too, usually based on how long they have been fermented. White and yellow miso are milder, while red is much stronger.

Parmesan Rinds

While keeping cheese in your fridge is perhaps an obvious thing to do, a very key step is to save your Parmesan rinds whenever you get to the end of your block of cheese and store them in a sealed container in the freezer. These can be added to pots of beans or soups, where they add wonderful aroma and flavor, and also become soft, tender, and fully edible. Saving your Parmesan rinds is a great reason to encourage buying higher quality Parmesan cheese (Parmigiano-Reggiano), rather than a rind-free version found in many supermarkets.

Sauerkraut

Sauerkraut, as I stated earlier in this intro, is literally just cabbage and salt that has been allowed to ferment. It is bright, crunchy, probiotic, very healthful, and a lot more versatile than you might think. It's actually very easy to make yourself, if you are so inclined. But it also happens to last for a *very* long time in the fridge. While it is of course great on a sausage or a hot dog, I use it frequently in dishes like Krauty Beans (page 138), Krauty Omelet (page 30), and Krauty Smoked Cheddar Broccoli Bread (page 67).

Helpful Kitchen Tools

There are a lot of kitchen gadgets out there, and the truth is that a great many of them will just end up sitting in a drawer, where their main purpose is to be pushed around while you look for a wine opener. So here I present an incomplete list of things that I find to be extremely functional.

KITCHEN TIPS

Don't wait to freeze leftovers until they are *about* to go bad—then all you're doing is pausing it at the last possible moment, when it's right on the edge. Be smart about it. When you make chicken stock, or too much sauce for Turkey Pasta (page 97), transfer it to a deli container, let it cool completely, label it, and freeze it.

When you freeze things in deli containers, remember that water *expands* when it freezes. So leave some extra room at the top of the container, otherwise it will swell up and knock the lid off in the freezer, which kind of defeats the purpose of sealing it in the first place.

Blenders, Stick Blenders, and Food Processors

Smoothies, tomato sauces, pestos, and dips are all things made much more easily with the use of some kind of machine that blends them up. (I do not recommend trying to make a smoothie with a mortar and pestle.) I tend to find that wetter mixtures (like smoothies) are happier in a standard blender or NutriBullet, while thicker ones with a coarser texture (like pestos), prefer food processors. Meanwhile, I love to use a stick/immersion blender if I want to blend something directly in the pot—like a blended tomato sauce, or even a pureed soup.

Deli Containers, Blue Tape, and Sharpies

This is a very restaurant-y thing to recommend, but I use these all the time. I buy half-pint, pint, and quart deli containers and reuse them regularly. They are dishwasher-safe, freezer-safe, and not so expensive that you feel bad about giving away leftovers in them. The other key to this is labeling your food with masking tape (usually blue, because that's what I was taught in restaurants) and a Sharpie—I always put the date on it so that I know when it was made and what it is. No matter how confident I am that I'll remember . . . I always forget.

A Good Knife, a Good Cutting Board

You don't need a whole set of knives. You need a good chef's knife (usually about 8 inches), a decent paring knife, and a good serrated (or bread) knife. That's honestly it. Everything else just gets in the way, unless you have very specific needs. Your chef's knife is worth splurging on—just make sure to test it out and know that it feels nice in your hand. Try to think of what you use it for, too. Japanese knives tend to be better for more precise knife work, while Western knives are better for more do-it-all chopping (and say, butchering a chicken). Buy one nice knife, take good care of it, and keep it sharp.

Which leads me to: a good cutting board. A good board will not only feel nicer to cut on, but it will also preserve the blade. I like a wooden cutting board, treated every few weeks with mineral oil so that it doesn't crack or absorb the flavors of things like garlic and onion.

Graters and Zesters

Remember that note about grating your own cheese? Well, it really, really helps when you have a nice box grater. It also works quite well to grate things like carrots or cabbage for salad. Additionally, I love having a Microplane zester for citrus, as well as for a finer grate on ingredients like ginger and garlic. (Some people swear by having one zester for garlic and ginger, and another for citrus.)

Kitchen Scale

Kitchen scales have gotten very affordable over the years, and I highly recommend keeping a digital one around for your cooking needs. Weight is *so much more* precise than volume (cups), particularly when dealing with ingredients like flour, sugar, and the like. You'll also find that it's cleaner and faster, too, once you get the hang of it. I try to go with the more convenient option of measure in all recipes, unless I *really* want you to weigh it, in which case I will list both weight and volume.

A NOTE ON GRAMS You will notice that all dough- and batter-based recipes in this book will have measurements listed in grams as well as cups (and teaspoons and tablespoons). For baking, grams are *far* more precise than teaspoons, cups, and ounces, and are the recommended method for measuring.

Kitchen Shears (aka Poultry Shears)

These are just heavy-duty scissors, but once I bought a pair, I discovered that I use them a lot more often than I thought I would. While it is the perfect tool for breaking down a chicken, I also often use them when I just want to snip a few herbs onto something, or cut up some large lettuce leaves in a bowl. In my lazier moments, when I don't feel like dirtying a cutting board, I have even used it to cut a quesadilla, or even a sandwich, directly on a plate.

A Mandoline

I don't have the best knife skills in the world—but sometimes I still want some really consistently sliced onions, potatoes, squash, or cabbage. This is where a mandoline comes in really handy—it is a real time-saver for things like coleslaw or gratins, while also making for a much more consistent outcome. You also don't need a fancy, French metal one—the simple Japanese plastic ones work really well. Just be *extremely* careful about cutting your fingertips. Don't be a hero. When you get to the end of a vegetable, just move on, or use a knife to slice it by hand.

Mason Jars

Mason jars aren't just for drinking water in your first apartment—they are also incredibly helpful as storage containers for things like pickles, smoothies, salad dressing, Ghee (page 18), Chile Oil (17), an open container of crackers, and anything else that you want to store with a little more substance and visual appeal than a deli container. Pro tip: Rather than the standard metal lids, buy some reusable, leakproof, plastic screw-top lids. They will hold up way longer than the metal ones (which are really just for shelf-stable pickling) and won't rust.

A Salad Spinner

Stop buying lettuce, spinach, and greens in plastic bags and boxes. The plastic is a *massive* waste issue, and it is almost never recyclable. What's more, you are dramatically limiting the quality and variety of the greens you are eating. There is so much more out there in terms of types of lettuces and greens, both at the grocery store and at farmers markets. There are endless flavors and textures that you are missing out on by avoiding anything that wasn't bleached in a processing facility and stuffed into a plastic bag.

But if you don't have a salad spinner, it makes washing and drying a lot more complicated. So if you get in the habit of buying bunches of greens, washing and then drying them in a salad spinner before you eat them, the quality of your meals will dramatically increase.

GREENS WASHING TIP

I like to prep the greens before I wash them. If it's Swiss chard, collard greens, or even lettuce that I want to chop, I cut it first (and remove the stems and midribs if necessary), then transfer them to a large pot of cold water (or the base of your salad spinner). From there, the leaves will float, and you can agitate them with your fingers and let them sit in the water. The dirt will naturally fall to the bottom of the pot. Then you simply lift them out of the pot with your fingers and lay them directly into the strainer basket in your salad spinner. After that, they are ready to spin until dry.

I also tend to wash greens as needed (or up to a day in advance with sturdier greens), since washed greens tend to spoil much faster.

Charred Vegetables with Spiced Labneh, page 56

pantry prep

(things to make and keep on hand)

A Pot of Beans

Makes 5 to 6 cups

Beans are one of the great sustainable, nutritious foods on the planet, filled with protein, fiber, vitamins, and minerals. While I always keep canned beans at the ready, I greatly prefer to cook a pot of beans from scratch, which usually results in a better bean that costs less money (with the added benefit of flavoring them however you see fit).

Additionally, you will start to discover different types of beans, and higher quality beans. Some of my favorites come from Rancho Gordo, a company that focuses on growing heirloom varietals of exceptional quality and beauty, while also supporting growers across North America, as well as working with small farms in Mexico to produce rare crops.

There are many ways to cook beans, but over the years I have landed on this oven method as my absolute favorite for creating an even, gentle cook with perfect results (though I have included a stovetop method as well). I also think that soaking your beans in advance is a waste of time that does not produce a higher quality cook, nor does it "de-gas" the beans, an urban myth that has been debunked by people far smarter than me.

- - -

1 pound **dried beans**, rinsed and sorted for small rocks

About 7 cups **water**

Salt

EQUIPMENT Ovenproof pot with a heavy lid (I use a 4½-quart Dutch oven)

Oven Method Preheat the oven to 325°F.

In an ovenproof pot with a lid (such as a Dutch oven), combine the beans, water, and a healthy pinch of salt (you are looking for about 2 inches of water above the beans). Bring the pot to a boil on the stove and taste the water for seasoning—it should be seasoned like a mellow broth. Cover the pot and transfer it to the oven.

Bake until fully tender all the way through, 1½ to 2½ hours. The cooking time can really vary, depending on the type of beans and how old they are. Also keep an eye on the water level, as if there is too little water, the beans will not fully cook. You always want to keep at least an inch of liquid above the beans.

If the beans seem *very* close to being done, you can turn off the oven and let them finish in the residual heat. Let them cool completely before storing them in the refrigerator. Store the beans completely submerged in their cooking liquid.

Stovetop Method In a Dutch oven, combine the beans, water, and a healthy pinch of salt (you are looking for about 2 inches of water above the beans). Bring the pot to a boil on the stove and taste the water for seasoning—it should be seasoned like a mellow broth. Cover the pot and keep it at a bare simmer on the stove, stirring occasionally, until the beans are fully tender all the way through, 1½ to 2½ hours. The cooking time can really vary, depending on the type of beans and how old they are. Keep an eye on the water level, as if there is too little water, the beans will seem to never fully cook. You always want to keep at least an inch of liquid above the beans.

Let them cool completely before storing them in the refrigerator. Store the beans completely submerged in their cooking liquid.

BEAN VARIATIONS

While I often cook my beans with just water and salt so that they will hold up well in any number of applications, sometimes I add a few other ingredients, just to impart extra flavor.

Try adding ingredients like these, in any combination, right at the beginning with the cold water:

Leek tops (the tough, green tops, thoroughly washed)
An **onion** or a pair of **shallots**, peeled and halved
A head of **garlic**, halved horizontally
A few **sprigs fresh herbs**, like rosemary, thyme, or parsley,
    tied together with kitchen twine
A **bay leaf**
A fresh **chile**, halved lengthwise
A **Parmesan rind**
Olive oil or **lard**

If you want to add a piece of meat, I recommend a smoked ham hock (the greatest bean meat) or any end of flavorful meat that you have on hand, like a prosciutto heel. But I'll add one caveat, via my friend and mentor Kevin Bludso: If you are adding meat, let it simmer for about an hour before adding the beans (though you can put the aromatic vegetables in there with the meat, too, if you like). The reason being that you want the water to take on the flavor of the meat, like a stock, *before* it begins absorbing into the beans. Stock takes longer to make than beans do, so let that flavor really develop.

Chicken Stock

A Philosophical Treatise That Also Includes a Recipe

An 8-quart stockpot will yield 3 to 4 quarts of stock

A 16-quart stockpot will yield 7 to 8 quarts of stock

Homemade chicken stock is one of the greatest things in the world—a golden nectar, extracting the truest essence from spare chicken parts and vegetable bits and transferring their properties into liquid form. Having it on hand means you can make a quick soup for yourself with deep, satisfying flavors, like Jewish Italian Chicken Noodle Soup (page 133), Ginger-Cilantro Chicken Noodle Soup (page 134), Shrimp Soupy Rice (page 128), or any number of recipes beyond the ones in this book.

Canned or boxed chicken broth is a woefully inadequate facsimile that has gradually and relentlessly made people forget what the real stuff is supposed to taste like. They often contain sodium, sugar, and "dehydrated chicken," as well as vegetable juice concentrates and yeast extract. They also, in almost all instances, contain an ingredient simply listed as "chicken broth." (What if you bought a bottle of ketchup and the first ingredient was "ketchup"?) I did a lot of research on this subject for an article that has grown ever more complex (and may never actually be completed). What I discovered, for the most part, is that boxed and canned broths start with a broth concentrate, made by a multinational corporation (they often describe their product as a "turnkey broth solution") that then sells it to different consumer-facing companies (these are the "brands" you've heard of) that then add their own flavorings and water to it to make it their own special "recipe." But basically, if you're buying any stock or broth in a box or a can, there is a very high probability that it is made by one of three gigantic multinational corporations that you have never heard of before.

Now look—I totally get that making real chicken stock takes up time that many of us don't have. But in truth, it's very simple: You simmer bones and vegetables for a few hours in some water and then you strain it. Personally, I find it to be a calm and meditative experience that does not require your full attention—something you can do when you have a day off at home. It is a down payment on your future meals and makes your house smell like a home. I always make a big batch, then transfer it into 1-quart deli containers and freeze whatever I don't plan on using within the next few days. Then whenever I want some, I can set it in the fridge the day before to thaw. Or I just run the container under cold water to loosen it up and then dump it into a pot, cover, and let it melt over medium heat. You can also pour your stock into ice cube trays and freeze it, then transfer the cubes to freezer bags.

Great chicken stock makes even the simplest dishes taste outstanding.

Some quick notes on making stock:

- Use the biggest pot you have on hand. I fill my largest pot up about 60 percent of the way with chicken bones and then I fill the rest of it up with water.
- You can use any chicken bones, like necks and backs, or even the carcass of a leftover roast chicken. You can also mix and match. I like to mix in some chicken feet if I can get my hands on them—they have extra collagen and bring a wonderful richness and body to the stock. →

- ← • I always keep a freezer bag going with various spare backbones or roast chicken carcasses that I will eventually use to make stock.
- You can also use whole chicken pieces, or even a whole chicken cut up into pieces. The meat will give more flavor to the broth; you can then pull the meat off the bones at the end for other uses.
- I tend to use a classic combination of celery, carrot, onion, peppercorns, and parsley stems, but you can modify to fit your taste. Garlic can be nice, or ginger. I often use the tough green tops of leeks, too. If you want your stock to be darker, you can leave the onion skins on the onions.
- Some people roast their raw bones to give color to the stock as well, but I prefer a lighter, clearer, more nuanced hay-colored stock.

Chicken bones, pieces, and **carcasses**: 4 pounds for an 8-quart stockpot; 8 to 9 pounds for a 16-quart stockpot

A few **celery stalks** with their leaves, washed and broken in half

A couple of **carrots**, washed and broken in half

An **onion**, halved and peeled, or the tough green top from a few leeks

A few **peppercorns**

A handful of **parsley stems**

EQUIPMENT Heavy-bottomed stockpot with a lid (the bigger the pot, the better), fine-mesh sieve, cheesecloth (optional), and 1-quart deli containers

Place the chicken bones and pieces in a large stockpot and fill the pot with water—leaving about 1½ inches of space at the top for bubbling: 4 to 5 quarts for an 8-quart stockpot and 8 to 9 quarts for a 16-quart stockpot. Bring to a boil—this will agitate the chicken bones and start releasing some foamy scum. Let it boil for about 5 minutes, reducing the heat if it is boiling too aggressively. After 5 minutes, reduce the heat to a very gentle simmer, then take a ladle and gently lower it into the pot to scoop up all of the scummy foam and throw it away.

Keep the pot at a bare simmer for about 2 hours (boiling too much will evaporate most of the water out). After 2 hours, add the vegetables, peppercorns, and parsley stems. At this point you can cook the stock at a lower heat, uncovered, so that it is barely bubbling at all—but the pot should be so hot that you cannot hold your finger on the outside of it for longer than a second.

Continue cooking the stock for at least 2 more hours, or as long as you are interested in doing it. I have friends who cook chicken stock for 18 hours, but truthfully, I usually only leave mine on the stove for about 6 hours. The good thing, though, is that if you are busy, you can just check on it from time to time and leave it be for as long as you want.

Once you think the stock is where you want it, ladle a little of it into a mug and season it with salt. If you are happy with the taste and texture, it is ready.

I will often use tongs to lift out and discard as many bones and scraps as I can before straining. If you have cheesecloth, use it to line a sieve and set the sieve over another pot or bowl, and ladle the stock into the sieve. (Or simply pour the stock slowly into an unlined sieve.) The goal is to be somewhat gentle so that the weight of the liquid doesn't push impurities through the sieve. Leave behind and discard any sediment at the bottom of the stockpot.

You can, if you are inclined, rinse the stockpot and then strain the stock one more time back into the pot.

To remove excess fat (especially from a stock that used a lot of chicken feet, or a roasted chicken carcass), allow the pot of stock to settle for a few minutes, then gently lower a ladle so that it just barely breaks through the surface of the liquid. The fat, having risen to the top, will fall into the ladle. Continue this until you've removed most of the fat from the stock. Alternatively, you can wait until the stock is refrigerated or frozen and then simply scoop it out (it will be opaque and look quite different from the rest of the stock).

Transfer the stock into containers and allow it to cool completely before storing it in the refrigerator or freezer.

PASTINA WITH CHICKEN BROTH

When I was little and got sick, my mom would sometimes make me a bowl of chicken broth with boiled pastina, orzo, or stars—though any tiny pasta shape will do. It is then finished with grated Parmesan cheese, salt, and black pepper. Simply boil the pasta separately from the stock, in salted water. Then heat the stock and season it to taste with salt. Drain the cooked pasta and add it to the bowl, adding the stock and topping it with cheese and black pepper.

It is, to this day, a deeply comforting thing to eat when I am sick, and also one of the purest ways to enjoy the virtues of excellent homemade chicken stock.

ESCAROLE AND WHITE BEAN SOUP

Along those same lines, escarole and white bean soup is another classic use for good chicken stock. This is something I make in the morning on Thanksgiving, because it is nutritious and light to eat a bit of throughout the day, without ruining my appetite for the big dinner.

Just set a few cups of chicken stock in a pot on the stove and then ladle in some cooked white beans, a handful of chopped escarole, and a Parmesan rind. Then simmer it all together for about 10 minutes, season it to taste with salt and pepper, and keep it warm on the stove, eating it whenever you feel inclined.

Vegan Dashi

Makes about 4 cups

Dashi is a broth that is the base of a lot of Japanese cooking. While there are many kinds of dashi, the most popular by far uses kombu (dried kelp) and katsuobushi (smoked fish shavings, also known as bonito flakes). But I often find myself making this simple, vegan version that uses just water, kombu, and dried mushrooms. You can even leave the mushrooms out entirely, though I find that I like the extra bit of earthy, umami punch that it gets.

I present two methods of this recipe—one is an overnight "cold brew" recipe in which you just let it all sit at room temperature for 8 to 10 hours. The faster (and only slightly less good) version involves the stove and takes about 10 minutes, but requires you to wash a pot.

After you have made dashi, the strained-out mushrooms and konbu can be used again (via the stovetop method) to make another batch of less nuanced dashi, called "secondary dashi." Think of it like that second, weaker cup of tea you can make with the same leaves you used for the first one.

On the whole, dashi (and secondary dashi) is a great base for soups or hot-pots, as a broth base for a bowl of noodles, or even an ingredient for reduced, simmered dishes like oyakodon (a chicken-and-egg rice bowl) or Dashi-Braised Sweet Potatoes (see page 11).

You can also chop up the rehydrated mushrooms and put them in soup or use them for Vegan Mapo Tofu (page 150). The kombu strips, meanwhile, have often been used by my wife as a face mask. Go figure.

....

4 cups **cold water**

1 (4-inch or so) square of **kombu** (or a few pieces equaling roughly that surface area)

¼ ounce **dried mushrooms**— any will do, but I most often use shiitake

Overnight Method Place the water in a 1-quart deli or similar-size container. Add the kombu and mushrooms, cover, and allow it to soak at room temperature for 8 to 10 hours. Strain the dashi and use it immediately or store it in the refrigerator for up to 5 days.

Stovetop Method In a saucepan, combine the water, kombu, and mushrooms. Set the pan over medium heat and bring it to a boil by gradually increasing the heat—the goal is for it to take about 10 minutes for the water to come to a boil. Once the water boils, immediately remove from the heat. Strain the dashi and use it immediately or store it in the refrigerator for up to 5 days.

VEGAN RICE SOUP

Just like the pastina with chicken stock, a bowl of any warm broth with small starchy things in it is very comforting to eat when you are sick. I stumbled upon this very simple combination of dashi, sauerkraut, and rice, which has no business being as delicious as it is.

Take 1½ cups Vegan Dashi (page 9) and place it in a pot with ½ cup chopped sauerkraut. Bring it to a simmer and then ladle it over cooked rice and season it to taste with salt and freshly ground black pepper.

DASHI-BRAISED SWEET POTATOES

This is a great, simple, classic Japanese side dish (it traditionally has sugar as well, though I prefer it without). Simply cut a sweet potato into bite-size pieces and place them in a small saucepot. Cover the sweet potatoes by an inch or so with dashi and add a splash of soy sauce. Increase the heat to a strong simmer, then cover the pot and allow it to keep simmering until the liquid is almost all reduced. If after about 20 minutes, the sweet potatoes are fully cooked and the broth has not reduced, you can remove the lid to reduce the liquid more quickly. Once it has reduced, turn the sweet potatoes into a bowl and pour any remaining reduced liquid over them. Eat as is, or with a squeeze of lemon and a sprinkle of shichimi.

A Perfect Egg

People often like to get very specific about their eggs. I usually try to keep some boiled eggs (in their shells) in the refrigerator for snacking, a quick breakfast, or to add to a bowl of ramen or Rice, Warm Greens, and Wilted White Cheddar (page 144). But how cooked should that egg be? That is up to you. The most important thing is learning how to make your eggs precisely how you like them, every single time.

I believe that this can be achieved by making your conditions as reproducible as possible. With this method, if you use the same brand and size of eggs, the same pot, and the same number of eggs every time, you will wind up with the same results.

I start with cold eggs straight from the fridge, then I lower them gently into boiling water and set a timer. (Some people believe in bringing their eggs to room temperature first, but I think that takes too long and, also, room temperature can really vary.)

When that timer is up, I pull them out and plunge them directly into an ice bath. The ice bath halts the cooking but also, I'm fairly certain, makes them easier to peel. Of course, if you want to eat them while they are hot you can pull them out as soon as they are cool enough to handle—I often eat one right away, then I let the rest cool in the ice bath before storing them in the refrigerator.

I prefer a large egg with a cooked white and a slightly runny, custardy yolk—about 7 minutes 30 seconds in the boiling water. Iliza likes hers to be closer to 9 minutes, so that the yolk is not runny, but hasn't turned chalky and pale yet either. At 11 minutes you will get a dry yolk, while a 6-minute egg will be fully runny.

The point here is: Variables change things—things like the altitude, the size of the eggs, the size of the pot, and the amount of water. But once you find the cook time that you prefer, in your kitchen and with your pot, you can make your eggs the way you like them, every single time.

As for the pot—a 4-quart saucepan is about as small as I would use for a dozen eggs. If you have a pasta pot with a perforated insert, this is ideal, since you can use it to lower the eggs into the water gently and then lift them out.

....

A dozen **eggs** (or as many as you want to cook)

EQUIPMENT Decent-size pot (at least 4 quarts if you are going to make a dozen eggs), slotted spoon or pasta insert to lower them into and lift them out of the water, and a large bowl

Fill a pot with enough water to fit your eggs in a single layer with at least 1½ inches of water above them. Bring the water to a boil over high heat. Once boiling, take the eggs from the refrigerator and lower them gently (but quickly) into the water and immediately start a timer. Give them a tender stir, then cover the pot until it returns to a boil.

While they are cooking, fill a large bowl with ice and cold water. When the timer goes off, immediately lift the eggs from the boiling water and plunge them directly into the ice water.

Allow them to chill for at least 15 minutes before draining and transferring to the refrigerator.

BONUS TIP If you have any plants that need watering, I often use the egg water and the ice bath water, once they have returned to room temperature. People say egg water is very good for plants.

Cal-Italian Pork Sausage
with Rosemary and Orange Zest

Makes about 1 pound

This is an uncased sausage—meaning that you're really just taking ground pork and mixing it with spices and seasonings. The truth is that I cook with uncased sausage a lot more frequently than I do ones in casings. This is a bright, California twist on a classic Italian pork sausage (devoid of sugar but loaded with flavor) that beautifully complements dishes like Broccoli-Sausage Bread (page 64), Broccoli-Sausage Pasta (page 102), and White Beans and Sausage with Kale (page 141). It is also great as a pizza topping.

Italian sausage from the grocery store is wildly inconsistent in terms of quality, and making your own mix is easy (it's only stuffing sausage into casings that is the hard part). I think that this is also a great way to start buying an affordably priced product from a higher end butcher with responsibly raised meat—and the result is not just more ethical, it is more delicious, too.

This recipe doubles and triples well, and the sausage can be frozen raw in an airtight container and kept for several months.

1 pound freshly ground **pork**

1 medium or 2 small **garlic cloves**, finely chopped

1 teaspoon **salt**

¼ teaspoon freshly ground **black pepper**

⅛ teaspoon **crushed red pepper**, or more to taste

1 teaspoon finely chopped **rosemary**

½ teaspoon **extra-virgin olive oil**

½ teaspoon grated **orange zest**

This is truly one of the easiest recipes in the book. Simply combine all of the ingredients in a medium or large bowl and mix them together thoroughly with your hands, folding and turning quickly until everything is completely incorporated.

This can be used right away but is slightly better after being left to incorporate for an hour or two. Store in a tightly covered container in the refrigerator. Cook it within 3 days, or else freeze it while raw and allow it to thaw completely before cooking.

Charred Tomatillo Salsa

Makes about 1 pint

Tomatillos are a staple of Mexican cuisine and native to the Americas, frequently used in salsa verdes and braises. This firm little green fruit gets soft when cooked and can then be blended into a bright, acidic salsa that I just love. One of my missions in this book is to get people to realize how easy tomatillos are to cook with, and how wonderful they are as an addition to almost anything you're eating.

This is a recipe for an incredibly simple, versatile salsa, to be used on Green Rice and Black Beans (page 148), dolloped onto your morning eggs, or eaten with a bag of tortilla chips. I love to char the tomatillos in the oven, which adds some blackened flecks and smoky flavor.

NOTE I love this salsa with dried chiles de árbol, which give a dry heat to contrast with the acid. For reference on this recipe:

1 chile de árbol = medium

2 chiles de árbol = hot

3 chiles de árbol = extra hot

NOTE 2 If you don't want to use your oven, you can simply boil the tomatillos until soft and sauté the garlic and chile in oil. Or, if you happen to have a smoker, I highly recommend tossing the tomatillos in there with some pecan wood (they take smoke flavor *extremely* well).

....

1 pound **tomatillos**, husked and rinsed

2 **garlic cloves**, peeled

2 teaspoons **neutral oil**, such as grapeseed, vegetable, or canola

Salt

1 to 3 **chiles de árbol** (see Note) or any dried red chile or crushed red pepper

EQUIPMENT Baking dish or a sheet pan lined with foil (large enough to fit the tomatillos in a single layer) and a blender or immersion blender

Set the broiler to high (or if you don't have a broiler, simply set your oven to as hot as it will go). Line a baking dish or sheet pan with foil.

Meanwhile, in a medium bowl, combine the tomatillos, garlic, oil, and a sprinkle of salt. Toss them to combine and then dump them into the lined baking dish or sheet pan. Place them in the oven one rack below the very top.

Broil (or roast) the tomatillos for 5 minutes, then flip them over and return them to the oven until the tomatillos are charred in spots and soft to the touch, like water balloons, and all of the bright green color has turned to a dark, khaki green.

Once cooked, transfer the tomatillos, garlic, and any collected juices to a blender (or back into the bowl if using an immersion blender).

Turn off the oven, place the chile(s) on the baking sheet, and immediately place in the oven. Toast the chile(s) in the residual heat until fragrant, about 2 minutes (if you are using crushed red pepper, you only need to toast them for about 15 seconds). Add the chile(s) to the blender or bowl, along with 1 tablespoon water (this will help open up the flavor, like with a nice whiskey). Blend the tomatillos until you have a smooth sauce. Taste the salsa for seasoning—it should be quite flavorful. Add more salt as needed.

Allow the salsa to cool to room temperature and then store, covered, in the refrigerator for 5 to 7 days.

Chile Oil

Makes about 1 cup

Chile oil is a wonderful thing to keep within arm's reach. It is great in a stir-fry, atop some Veggie Scrap Fried Rice (page 149), as the oil base for Vegan Mapo Tofu (page 150), or combined with some soy sauce and rice vinegar as a dip for dumplings.

There are many ways to make chile oil, but this one has become my favorite. Here you almost confit the chiles, garlic, and ginger submerged in oil and over slow, low heat. Then you strain the oil and pour it over some crushed dried chiles. I keep the flavorings fairly simple, but if you want to add spices like star anise, cinnamon, or even a handful of chopped scallions, it is certainly not a bad idea.

If you want to make a chile oil with a deeper color, add ½ teaspoon ground turmeric, paprika, or ground annatto along with the garlic and ginger.

Chile oil will keep for about 4 months at room temperature, or much longer in the refrigerator.

½ ounce (about ⅔ cup) whole **dried chiles** (I prefer chiles de árbol, but any dried red chiles will work)

1 teaspoon **cumin seeds**

1 cup **neutral oil** (I prefer peanut, but canola, vegetable, or grapeseed all work well)

2 **garlic cloves**, thinly sliced

1-inch or so knob fresh **ginger**, sliced

A pinch of **salt**

¼ teaspoon **crushed red pepper** or ground red chiles

EQUIPMENT Small heavy-bottomed saucepan, heatproof storage container (like a ½-pint mason jar), and a sieve

In a small heavy-bottomed saucepan, roast the chiles and cumin seeds over medium-low heat until they are just fragrant, about 2 minutes. Add the oil, garlic, ginger, and salt and reduce the heat to low. Eventually, as the oil comes up to temperature, you will begin to see bubbles forming around the garlic and ginger and rising to the surface. Continue cooking it at a low heat until the garlic has turned pale brown and is completely soft—this usually takes about 15 minutes. Remove from the heat once this is achieved and let it sit for another 5 minutes.

Meanwhile, place the crushed red pepper in the bottom of a 1-pint mason jar (or other heatproof container). Pour the oil into a sieve set over the jar (discard the solids).

Allow the oil to come to room temperature before screwing on the lid. Store it at room temperature or in the refrigerator.

Ghee

Makes about 1½ cups

Ghee is a very popular, delicious, and highly useful clarified butter that originated in India and is used all over the world. To make it, butter is cooked gently, and then the milk solids are separated out and removed. The result is a wonderfully aromatic fat that has a much higher smoke point—put simply: a higher temperature at which the fat will smoke and burn—making ghee perfect for frying and browning. Plus, removing all the milk solids means ghee is considered safe to consume if you are lactose intolerant, and also makes a product that will last for several months.

It is a wonderful ingredient to use if you are making Shantam's Kitchari (page 36), Shichimi Popcorn (page 46), or even just to sear things like chicken or steak, as it creates a golden brown surface with very little burning.

I prefer a light yellow, golden hue for my ghee, but some people prefer a nuttier, darker brown version—to achieve this, simply cook the ghee even longer. The key is to keep the temperature low so that you do not burn the milk solids and turn the whole thing bitter.

NOTE It takes about 45 minutes to 1 hour to make ghee, but it is a mostly inactive process. If you find that you use ghee a lot, I recommend doubling this recipe to save on time in the long run.

1 pound **unsalted butter**

EQUIPMENT Narrow heavy-bottomed saucepan, spoon or ladle, fine-mesh sieve, cheesecloth (optional), and 1-pint mason jar

In a narrow heavy-bottomed saucepan, melt the butter over medium-high heat. Once the butter has melted, reduce the heat to low or medium-low, depending on the strength of your stove. Keep the butter on low heat and do not stir it—simply use a spoon or ladle to gently remove any impurities that form at the surface and discard them. Continue cooking the ghee until it has turned quite translucent, 45 minutes to 1 hour.

Continue cooking for a darker, nuttier ghee, or simply remove it from the heat and allow it to sit for about 10 minutes to allow the milk solids to settle to the bottom.

Set a fine-mesh sieve or double layer of cheesecloth over the mouth of a mason jar and slowly pour in the ghee, leaving any solids that have separated in the bottom of the pan. Allow the ghee to come down to room temperature, then cover and transfer to the refrigerator, where it will harden. Store the ghee for up to 9 months under refrigeration, or at room temperature for up to 3 months.

Mom's Pie Crust

Makes enough for 2 pie crusts

This is the pie crust I grew up on. It is flaky, crumbly, and fairly universal—wonderful for everything from strawberry rhubarb pie, to savory things, like the Gruyère, Leek, and Swiss Chard Pie (page 61).

This dough is best used within a couple of days of making it. But you can also freeze the dough for up to 6 months—though I would recommend rolling it out into a flat disc and tightly wrapping it in plastic before you freeze it.

If you are using the dough right after you make it, refrigerating it for 1 hour before rolling out is ideal.

I prefer to use a food processor, but this can also be mixed by hand.

2 sticks (8 ounces/225g) **unsalted butter**

2½ cups (335g) **all-purpose flour**

1 teaspoon (7g) **fine sea salt**

1 teaspoon (5g) **sugar**

½ cup or so of **ice water**

EQUIPMENT Food processor or large bowl, pastry cutter or forks, and plastic wrap

Cut the butter into 1-inch or so pieces and then refrigerate or freeze to get them as cold as possible.

In a food processor (or in a large bowl), combine the flour, salt, and sugar. Blend (or whisk) everything together so that they are fully combined.

Once the ice water is quite cold, remove the ice and discard it (just make sure you don't drop ice cubes into your dough) and take the butter out of the fridge or freezer.

Food Processor Method Add the butter to the flour mixture, as well as 1 teaspoon of the ice water, and blend the mixture. With the machine running, add ice water about 1 teaspoon at a time, letting the machine run for 10 seconds after each addition, until the dough begins to come together—it will often come together after just a moment of blending. Once the dough begins to collect into a single ball and rolls around the food processor, you can stop blending. The dough should be able to hold its shape to the touch without crumbling, while also not being tacky or wet. If it is too wet, add a sprinkle of flour and blend again. If it is too dry, add another teaspoon of water.

Hand Mixing Method Add the butter to the flour mixture, as well as 1 teaspoon of the ice water, then mix it with a pastry cutter or two forks—trying to break up the butter as much as possible and create a sandy, consistent texture. Once the butter is incorporated, shape the dough into a ball, being careful not to overwork it and warm it with your hands. The dough should be able to hold its shape to the touch without crumbling, while also not being tacky or wet. If it is too wet, add a sprinkle of flour and blend again. If it is too dry, add another teaspoon of water.

Once you have completed the dough, turn it out onto a surface and shape it into a round dough ball, then press it down from the top, being careful to touch it as little as possible so that the heat of your hands doesn't soften the dough. Cut it in half and place each piece on a piece of plastic wrap.

Wrap each piece of dough in plastic and then press it down into a disc about ¼ to ⅝ inch thick. Press together any cracks around the edges of the dough. Place the dough discs in the refrigerator to chill for at least 1 hour before rolling. If you want to freeze the dough, you can roll it into a thin disc, wrap it tightly in plastic, and transfer it to the freezer.

Nearly Pizza Dough

Makes two 9-ounce (260g) balls

I take pizza dough very seriously, and think of pizza as an infinity rabbit hole—a practice in which you can strive endlessly for perfection while knowing that it is unattainable, attempting to strike the delicate balance between science and chaos.

But then there is this dough—a very simple, quick one, whose job is simply to be flattened on your counter, filled with ingredients, and then rolled up and baked. It is the dough I use to make my mom's classic Broccoli-Sausage Bread (page 64), Krauty Smoked Cheddar Broccoli Bread (page 67), or any other haphazard creations I want to put together from things that happen to be sitting in the fridge.

This dough can be made in a stand mixer, but, truthfully, I tend to do it by hand. Once mixed, it proofs at room temperature for about 45 minutes and then is ready to use.

This recipe makes two balls of dough, so you can freeze one of them if you would like, but I always find it is nice to make two different breads and bake them at the same time. I recommend making the dough, then preparing your fillings while the dough is proofing.

As you can see, I put the gram weights first here. I highly recommend going by weight measurements rather than volume for this recipe, but both options will still work.

183g (¾ cup) **warm water** (100° to 110°F)

4g (½ to ¾ teaspoon) **honey**

1 envelope (7g/¼ ounce) **active dry yeast**

1 teaspoon **olive oil**

312g (2⅓ cups) **all-purpose flour**

8g (1 teaspoon) **fine sea salt**

EQUIPMENT Stand mixer fitted with a dough hook or a large mixing bowl

Pour the warm water into the bowl of a stand mixer (or a regular bowl). Add the honey and whisk it so that it mostly dissolves. Pour the yeast over the liquid and let it sit for about 10 minutes—or until the yeast begins to foam and bubble. If it does not activate after 15 minutes, your yeast may be dead, requiring you to start over with a fresher batch.

Once the yeast is ready, add the olive oil, flour, and salt. Knead the dough in the bowl (with a dough hook at medium-low speed, or by hand) until it comes together and forms a dough. Give a few minutes of solid kneading before deciding if it is too dry or too wet—it will probably come together. But if it is still flaking and crumbling, you can add more water, 1 teaspoon or so at a time. If it is still quite tacky and wet, you can add a bit more flour. You are looking for a dough that is similar to a New York–style pizza dough—which means that it should not stick too much to your hands or other surfaces, but be pliable and have some bounce to it.

If you are making the dough in a stand mixer, raise the speed to medium and allow it to knead until it has a smooth surface—about 8 minutes. If you are kneading by hand, transfer the dough ball to a clean surface and knead it until it starts to form a smooth surface, about 10 minutes. Return the dough to the bowl and cover it with plastic. Proof the dough until it doubles in size, 35 minutes to 1 hour, depending on the temperature of your room.

Cut the dough evenly in half. If you are not using the dough right away, wrap it tightly and keep it in the refrigerator. Just allow it to sit at room temperature for at least 30 minutes before baking with it. Or if you are using only one dough ball, tightly wrap the other one and keep it in the refrigerator or freezer.

This dough will freeze fairly well for 3 to 4 months.

breakfast

(at any hour)

← Forest Floor Oatmeal, page 26

Blender Batter Yogurt Pancakes

Or: How I Learned to Make Gluten-Free Pancakes Using Just a Blender and a Skillet

Makes 10 to 12 pancakes

I really like buckwheat pancakes—my favorite version of them is from Marion Cunningham's *Breakfast Book,* in which they are yeasted (ideally the night before), which gives them a nice punchy sourness.

But truthfully, most people do not want to take the time to yeast their breakfast. So I wanted to see if I could come up with a version that was totally gluten-free, had some of that sour punch to it, and could be put together quite quickly. After a couple of experiments with the blender, I wound up with this: oats, buckwheat flour, yogurt, and a few other things, blended and then poured into a hot skillet. During my experiments, my mom and stepdad happened to be in the neighborhood and came by to try them, then promptly ate all of them and declared, "These are perfect, don't change them and send us the recipe." So here they are!

If such a thing appeals to you, fresh fruit, like blueberries, can be sprinkled onto the pancakes after you've put them on the pan or griddle.

NOTE While they do taste nice if cooked right away, I think these pancakes are slightly better when the batter has rested for about 15 minutes prior to cooking.

. . . .

¾ cup (75g) **rolled oats**

⅔ cup (125g) **buckwheat flour**

2 large **eggs**

1½ cups **plain yogurt**

½ teaspoon grated **lemon zest**

1 tablespoon fresh **lemon juice**

½ teaspoon **baking powder**

½ teaspoon **baking soda**

¼ teaspoon **fine sea salt**

½ teaspoon **vanilla extract**

1 teaspoon **honey**

For serving: **butter, maple syrup,** and **flaky sea salt**

EQUIPMENT Blender and a griddle or skillet

In a blender, combine the oats, buckwheat flour, eggs, yogurt, lemon zest, lemon juice, baking powder, baking soda, salt, vanilla, and honey. Blend until the mixture is fully combined—scraping down the sides of the blender if necessary, to dislodge any dry wheat clumps.

Heat a griddle or skillet over medium-high heat. Pour the batter into your desired size (I like to use about ⅓-cup scoop per pancake). The batter should bubble slightly. When it is browned on one side, use a spatula to flip it over and press it down gently to make sure that the whole of the pancake makes contact with the heating surface.

Once each pancake is browned on the second side and cooked through, transfer it to a plate and garnish it with the unimpeachable trio of butter, maple syrup, and salt.

Forest Floor Oatmeal

Serves 1, but you can easily scale it up for as many as needed

In my continued crusade to remove sugar from the American breakfast, I have found myself often making this oatmeal, which removes the criminally unhealthy combination of brown sugar and maple syrup from your oats and replaces them with crunchy, salty, butter-kissed almond slices, coconut shreds, and chia seeds. The soft oatmeal gets served with a crispy golden brown layer that looks, to my mind, like a forest floor. A dollop of cold plain yogurt brings a tart, hot-and-cold contrast, allowing you to dip back and forth between the textures and temperatures.

Can you drizzle a little honey or maple syrup over the top if you are so inclined? Well, yes—I'm not in charge of your breakfast. But try it without first (it is very good) and see if you miss it.

½ cup **rolled oats**

¼ cup sliced **almonds**

¼ cup **unsweetened coconut flakes**

½ teaspoon **chia seeds**

1 tablespoon **unsalted butter**

Salt

Dollop of **plain yogurt**

EQUIPMENT Pot for cooking the oats and a skillet

In a small pot, cook the oats according to the package directions.

Meanwhile, heat a skillet over medium heat until it's warm to the touch. Add the sliced almonds and toast them in the dry pan, stirring the pan occasionally, for 90 seconds. Add the coconut and chia seeds and continue toasting them, stirring frequently, until they are all toasted and golden brown, 3 to 4 minutes longer.

Once they are toasted, remove from the heat, add the butter and a pinch of salt, and stir the mixture together until the butter is melted and has coated the rest of the ingredients. Set the pan aside.

Pour the oatmeal into your bowl. Scatter the crispy almond/coconut/chia topping across the whole surface of the oatmeal. Add a dollop of cold yogurt to the bowl and eat it immediately, adding more yogurt or salt as you see fit.

Farmers Market Breakfast

Serves 2

On Sunday mornings while my wife is still asleep, I often wander off to the Hollywood Farmers Market. This way, I can get the ingredients for our preferred Sunday breakfast. The precise type of greens or mushrooms or cheese vary depending on the trip, but it usually involves some eggs, lightly scrambled with a bit of soft goat cheese, eaten alongside some sautéed, barely wilted spinach or a similarly tender green, and some mushrooms that have been cooked in butter, tamari, and rosemary, and finished with a squeeze of lemon. A piece of toast rubbed with a clove of garlic, then buttered and sprinkled with salt, is not a bad addition either, but also not necessary.

I like to do everything in the same pan, and often prefer my vegetables at room temperature. But if you want a purer egg experience, you can of course cook your egg in a separate pan. An extremely slow-and-low soft scramble, or even runny fried eggs, make for great options here as well.

NOTE I actually use exactly this same preparation for the Mushroom and Spinach Bean Bowl (page 142), in case you are looking for a heartier, more wintry application of these vegetables.

3 tablespoons **unsalted butter**

2 sprigs **fresh rosemary**

1 tablespoon **tamari,** plus more to taste

8 ounces roughly torn **mixed mushrooms,** or any mushroom that you like (making sure that you remove any tough stems, like the ones on shiitakes)

1 tablespoon **olive oil,** plus more to finish

3 tablespoons finely chopped **shallots** (though you could substitute onions)

1 bunch (about 6 ounces) **spinach,** washed and relatively dry

¼ teaspoon **crushed red pepper**

Salt

½ **lemon**

4 large **eggs**

1 ounce **goat cheese** (or any cheese you like)

Freshly ground **black pepper**

EQUIPMENT Sauté pan or skillet

In a sauté pan or skillet, melt 2 tablespoons of the butter over medium heat. Once it is melted, add the rosemary sprigs and allow them to toast for about 30 seconds. Add the tamari and stir it to combine. Toss in the mushrooms and sauté, stirring occasionally, until they are fully cooked and tender, about 8 minutes, depending on the types of mushrooms you're using. Discard the rosemary stems (leave any leaves behind).

Divide the mushrooms between two serving bowls. Leave any extra liquid behind in the pan.

Return the pan to medium heat and add the olive oil and shallots. Sauté until just wilted, about 1 minute. Increase the heat to high, wait 30 seconds, then add the spinach and crushed red pepper. Season lightly with salt and stir constantly until the spinach is just wilted but not mushy, about a minute.

Spoon or dump the spinach next to the mushrooms, divided between the two bowls. Squeeze a bit of lemon over the vegetables.

Meanwhile, return the pan to the stove, reduce the heat to low, and add the remaining 1 tablespoon butter. Crack the eggs into a medium bowl and crumble in the goat cheese. Lightly beat the eggs, then add them to the pan, cooking your scrambled eggs as you most like them—I tend to like to tilt the pan and drag a silicone spatula across them, repeating the motion until you have long, fluffy strands of egg.

Season the eggs to taste with salt and pepper and plate them next to the vegetables (or allow the other diners to season their own eggs). Eat immediately.

Goat Cheese and Veggie Scrap Frittata

Serves 2 to 4

People tend to get very specific about their eggs and how they like them. But this frittata is meant to be somewhat utilitarian—easy to pull off, highly functional, and making use of some of those broccoli stems I tell you not to throw away in other parts of the book (cauliflower stems would work very well here, too). Those stems, supposedly, are even better for you than the florets, and since you're being charged by the pound anyway, it feels especially wasteful to throw them out. Also, while I like the softness of broccoli florets with pasta, I like the crunchiness of the stems with the texture of cooked eggs and soft goat cheese.

A frittata is something very different from, say, a soft French omelet. This is a heap of healthful, bonus vegetable scraps, held together by just a bit of egg, crisped and browned under the broiler and livened up with goat cheese and lemon zest.

You can eat this on its own as a breakfast for two, but I really like to cut it in quarters and serve it for lunch along with buttered toast and a light, leafy salad dressed with Shallot Vinaigrette (page 77).

2 tablespoons **olive oil**

2 **garlic cloves**, chopped

¼ teaspoon **crushed red pepper**, or to taste

About 2 cups roughly diced **broccoli** or **cauliflower stalks**

Salt and freshly ground **black pepper**

4 large **eggs**

2 ounces **goat cheese**

Grated zest of ½ **lemon**

EQUIPMENT 11-inch broiler-proof skillet (or something close enough in size—the wider the pan, the thinner the frittata) and a silicone spatula

Preheat the broiler to high.

In a broiler-proof skillet, heat the oil over medium heat until it is shimmering. Add the garlic and sauté until it is just softened, 1 to 2 minutes. Add the crushed red pepper flakes and allow them to toast for 30 seconds. Add the diced stems and season to taste with salt and black pepper. Continue to sauté, stirring occasionally, until they are tender, about 8 minutes.

Meanwhile, in a bowl, beat the eggs and a sprinkle of salt until unified.

When the vegetables are tender, remove the pan from the heat. Add the eggs and give the whole mixture a quick stir. Tilt the pan forward, backward, left, and right, allowing the eggs to fill in the gaps and make something of a round. Use the end of a silicone spatula to slide between the farthest edges of the egg and the pan, releasing any thin bits that are stuck to the walls, and let them fall down toward the rest of the frittata.

Dot the top of the frittata with the goat cheese, then sprinkle with the lemon zest and some freshly ground pepper.

Place the pan under the broiler for 1 to 2 minutes (depending on your broiler), just to cook until the eggs are set and the edges of the frittata have browned to your liking.

Using a potholder or kitchen towel, carefully remove the skillet from the oven. Give it a shake—it should slide about comfortably. Slide the frittata directly onto a cutting board. Cut into quarters and serve immediately.

Krauty Omelet

Serves 1

This is a quick, nutritious breakfast—a quite thin omelet, adorned with a scattering of bright, crunchy, fermented sauerkraut, which has been barely wilted and warmed through.

I have tried other versions, too—with caramelized onions and crispy kraut—but kept coming back to this version. It is simple and light. My favorite version uses homemade chile oil, for those who like a little heat.

1 tablespoon **unsalted butter, olive oil**, or **Chile Oil** (page 17)

2 large **eggs**, well beaten

¼ cup well-drained **sauerkraut**

Salt and freshly ground **black pepper**

EQUIPMENT 11-inch or so nonstick skillet (the wider the pan, the thinner the omelet) and a silicone spatula

In a nonstick skillet, heat the butter (or oil) over medium-low heat. Once the butter is melted (or the oil has spread across the bottom of the pan), add the beaten eggs and tilt the pan so that the egg reaches all the way to the edges.

Scatter the sauerkraut in a pleasing arrangement on top of the eggs. Season the omelet with salt and pepper (keeping in mind that the sauerkraut already has salt) and tilt the pan in a circular motion again so that any puddles of egg spread evenly throughout. Use a silicone spatula to gently lift the egg from the edges of the pan. Continue cooking, shaking the pan occasionally, until the eggs are just cooked through to your liking.

Slide the omelet onto a plate and eat it immediately.

Fruity, Nutty, Ginger-y Dessert Smoothie

Serves 1

Am I using the term "dessert" loosely? Why yes. But I really do find that this hits the spot when you're sitting on the couch watching TV and want *something* sweet to snack on, which you won't immediately regret having eaten. This requires no sugar or honey—it is just fruit and yogurt, made rich and nutty through the use of almond butter and chia seeds, with a whisper of a kick from the ginger. Iliza and I try to make this as thick as our blender will allow, only adding more liquid if absolutely necessary. We find that it is best enjoyed eaten from tiny cups with tiny spoons.

Obviously, this recipe can be doubled, tripled, or quadrupled, as you desire.

½ cup **plain yogurt** or **orange juice** (or a combination of both), plus more as needed

1 cup **frozen fruit**, such as strawberries, peaches, blueberries, and/or pineapple

½-inch knob fresh **ginger**

2 teaspoons **chia seeds**

2 tablespoons **salted almond butter** (or unsalted, plus a pinch of salt)

EQUIPMENT Blender

In a blender, combine all of the ingredients and blend until quite smooth, occasionally stirring or shaking the blender to get it to blend with as little liquid as you can manage—only adding a splash or so more as absolutely needed.

Transfer the smoothie to a cup and eat it with a spoon, or a reusable straw.

Health Sludge

Or: An Actually Complete Breakfast

Makes about 16 ounces (enough to serve 1 or 2)

Health Sludge is not here to be delicious. The goal is to take a large portion of your health and nutritional needs of the day and jam them into one chuggable smoothie. There is no fruit juice in Health Sludge, nor is there vanilla-flavored almond milk, or honey. The only liquid is water, and perhaps a splash of unsweetened probiotic kefir (which helps with gut health, and the little bit of fat also helps your body—along with the black pepper—to absorb the nutrients of the turmeric). Everything in Health Sludge is there exclusively for nutrition over flavor. With that being said, when you call something "Health Sludge," people tend to set incredibly low expectations and then try it and say things like, "You know what? It's actually not that bad."

This is the most common thing I eat for breakfast. As a result, I try to always keep some fresh greens on hand, or at worst, some frozen spinach or broccoli just in case. Treat this like your daily vitamins—knock them back quickly and then go about your day.

Of course, feel free to modify and adapt as needed. If you don't have time to wait for oats to bloom, you can go heavier on the chia and flax. Don't have flax? Double up on chia. As long as you are jamming healthful greens in there, you are getting the job done.

2 cups **water** (or 1½ cups **water** and ½ cup **unsweetened kefir** or **plain yogurt**)

½ cup **rolled oats**

1 tablespoon ground **flaxseeds** or 1½ tablespoons whole flaxseeds

1 tablespoon **chia seeds**

1 cup **frozen berries**, such as blueberries, strawberries, cranberries, or a mixture

2 cups loosely packed **healthful greens** or 1½ cups frozen greens

½ teaspoon ground **ginger powder** or a 1-inch knob fresh ginger

½ teaspoon ground **turmeric**

Twist of **black pepper**

EQUIPMENT Blender

In a blender, combine all of the ingredients and blend until quite smooth, adding more water if the mixture is thicker than you would prefer.

Transfer the blender to the refrigerator and allow it to sit for 15 minutes, letting the oats bloom in the liquid—which will also thicken the liquid, so if it is too thick after it has sat, you can add another splash of water, blend again, and then drink.

Golden Milk

Serves 1

Golden Milk is a combination of milk, water, and spices boiled together and then strained to create a beautifully colored beverage. It can be consumed at any time, but works quite well before you go to bed. This recipe comes from Ayurvedic practitioner and herbalist Keith Topar—a charming and thoughtful man who also, at one point, managed the café at the Mount Madonna Center, where my brother lived for many years.

I asked Keith for his distilled explanation of the properties of Golden Milk. He told me that "this concoction helps to uncover inner clarity and promotes an unhesitatingly responsible use of the mind. The ingredients in Golden Milk act to cooperatively bring warmth to the inner ecosystem and encourage overall balance. It builds strength in the nervous and immune systems and acts as a rejuvenative for the body-mind."

He also encourages the use of organic, grass-fed cow's milk of the highest quality, or a freshly made nut milk. If you tend to get congested, he recommends goat milk instead of cow. Lastly, if you are so inclined, raw honey and a few strands of saffron can be added to the cup with the Golden Milk (but they should not be boiled with the milk and the rest of the spices). Finally, Keith adds that "this drink can be enjoyed on its own or paired with a serving of dates."

1 cup **whole milk**

½ cup **water**

½ teaspoon **Golden Milk Spice Mix** (recipe follows)

EQUIPMENT Heavy-bottomed pot and a fine-mesh sieve

In a heavy-bottomed pot, combine the milk, water, and golden milk spice mix and bring to a boil over medium-high heat. Reduce the heat to a steady, gentle boil and stir the mixture. Simmer it for 3 minutes and then strain through a fine-mesh sieve into a mug and enjoy.

Golden Milk Spice Mix

Makes about 3½ tablespoons

4 teaspoons ground **turmeric**

3 teaspoons ground **cardamom**

2 teaspoons ground **ginger**

1 teaspoon ground **cinnamon**

¼ teaspoon ground **cloves**

¼ teaspoon ground **nutmeg**

Mix everything together and store in a screw-top jar.

Shantam's Masala Chai

Makes 2 servings

Tea did not become a popular beverage in India until the early twentieth century, when independent chaiwalas would make batches of chai and sell it from small, roadside stands. It has since become quite popular, most commonly made by boiling water and milk with freshly ground spices and then quickly steeped with rather a lot of cheap loose-leaf black tea, strained, and mixed with sugar.

This is the version that my brother makes (you will also find his Kitchari recipe in this book on page 36), and it is to be made quickly, using freshly ground spices, and then consumed immediately. It is also one of only two occurrences of sugar in this book, because it is actually an essential part of great chai, which is all about the balance of ginger, cardamom, and sugar, fortified with a heavy dose of caffeine. While "chai lattes" are popular and have many fans, they are made from concentrates and steamed milk. I encourage you to try this version instead.

I think it is best with whole milk, but you can certainly substitute oat, soy, or almond milk with fairly positive results—just be careful that they don't have any hidden sugars or flavorings. A splash of half-and-half at the end can be nice, too.

I really do prefer freshly ground spices, which make for a stronger, sharper flavor. It is better in the same way that freshly ground coffee is better than preground. In fact, I prefer to use a coffee grinder rather than a spice grinder, and do not at all mind if some remnant spices get into my coffee—nor if some remnant coffee grounds find their way into my chai.

---

2 cups **whole milk** (or soy, almond, or oat milk)

1 cup **water**

1 tablespoon plus 1 teaspoon **green cardamom pods**

¼ teaspoon **black peppercorns**

A roughly 1½-inch piece of **cinnamon**, whacked and broken up with the back of a knife

1½ tablespoons roughly chopped fresh **ginger**

2 tablespoons **loose-leaf black tea**, such as orange pekoe

2 tablespoons **granulated white sugar**

EQUIPMENT Medium pot, a coffee grinder, and a fine-mesh sieve or tea strainer

In a medium pot, combine the milk and water and set it over medium heat.

Meanwhile, place the cardamom, peppercorns, and pieces of cinnamon stick in the grinder and grind them into a fine powder.

Add the spices to the pot of milk and water along with the fresh ginger. Increase the heat to high, keeping an eye on it the whole time. Once it comes to a boil, immediately remove from the heat and add the black tea. Stir it frequently, watching the color until you have a camel brown hue.

Strain the tea through a fine-mesh sieve (or tea strainer) into a bowl. Add the sugar to the bowl of tea and stir to combine. Taste for sugar and add more if you would like. Pour it into cups and drink it immediately.

Shantam's Kitchari

Serves 2 or 3

Kitchari is a rice and lentil porridge very popular in much of India, often given to babies as an early solid food. There is a lot of personal variation in the way that people make, eat, and even pronounce (or spell) kitchari—but it is often made with some form of lentils, rice, and ginger, and spiced with turmeric, cumin seeds, and black mustard seeds that have been fried and toasted in ghee.

I started eating it a lot after my brother first moved to a place called Mount Madonna, up in the Santa Cruz Mountains—an intentional community and education center. My brother went on to live there for fifteen years, becoming a pujari of their Hanuman temple. Kitchari is a staple food that my brother eats most days up there, and it has become a regular meal in my kitchen, too.

So below I present my brother's version.

Once you make kitchari you can start to modify and experiment however you see fit. Sometimes I use brown rice instead of white, or whole mung beans instead of red lentils or split mung. Sometimes I will even take a handful of chopped greens like spinach and toss them into the pot at the very end before serving.

Kitchari can be reheated gently on the stove or in the microwave with just a little bit of water to help open it back up.

NOTE Asafoetida is a very common and distinctive spice in Indian cooking, though some people strongly dislike the smell on its own. I encourage you to try it and see how it enhances your dish. It is often said to aid in digestion, and has a uniquely savory and allium-like taste and aroma.

....

½ cup **dal** (lentils—ideally split yellow lentils or red lentils, known as toor dal or masoor dal, respectively)

½ cup **basmati rice**

2 tablespoons diced fresh **ginger**

2 tablespoons **Ghee** (page 18) or a neutral oil, such as canola, vegetable, or grapeseed

2 teaspoons **cumin seeds**

2 teaspoons **black mustard seeds** (or any mustard seed you have on hand)

Pinch of **asafoetida** (optional)

1 teaspoon ground **turmeric**

1 teaspoon ground **cumin**

Pinch of ground **cinnamon** (optional)

¼ teaspoon **kosher salt**

Wash the lentils and rice—my preferred way is to pour them into a sieve and then set the sieve in a large bowl of water and agitate them by hand to release as much as starch as possible. Then lift the sieve up and repeat with a fresh bowl of water. It will usually require 2 or 3 changes of water until it is mostly clear. Drain well.

Transfer the lentils and rice to a 4-quart or larger saucepan and add the ginger and 7 cups water. Bring to a boil, stirring occasionally. Reduce to a bare simmer, cover the pot, and cook until you end up with a soft and thoroughly cooked porridge that is not too dense or too watery. As it cooks, be careful of the starchy bubbles rising, escaping, and dribbling down the sides of the pot. Also keep an eye on the water level—lentils really like a lot of water to cook. If you find that the lentils and rice have absorbed most of the water but are not fully cooked, you should add more boiling water and give it a stir. The timing can vary quite a lot depending on the lentils—but 45 minutes is usually a pretty good rough guide. Overcooking is not a concern as long as there is enough water in the pot. Don't worry if you have added too much water either—if the kitchari seems fully cooked but a bit loose, you can continue simmering until it has the consistency of a medium-thick porridge. Once the kitchari is cooked, remove from the heat and keep it covered.

Meanwhile, in a small skillet or saucepan, heat the ghee over high heat. Add the cumin and mustard seeds. They will slowly begin to pop and fry—once they begin to pop with some frequency, add the asafoetida (if using). Once they have been popping for

Sliced fresh **cilantro**

Yogurt

Stewed fruit, such as
dates or raisins

Liquid aminos

Soy sauce

Tamari

An **Indian pickle,** like
mango or lime

Chutney or **jam**

Hot sauce

Tender greens

EQUIPMENT Sieve, saucepan or
pot (at least 4-quart) with a lid,
and a small skillet or saucepan

about 25 seconds, remove from the heat and add the turmeric, ground cumin, and cinnamon (if using), stirring the pan to combine the spices.

Uncover the kitchari and pour the ghee and spices right into the pot—they will sputter and fry as they hit it. Add the salt and stir everything together. Serve immediately, topped with the adornments of your choice.

Mom's Brown Rice Pudding

Serves 6 to 8

This was the only rice pudding I ate for the first twenty or so years of my life. When I finally tried "regular" pudding made with white rice, I thought it tasted like mushy, overly sweet baby food. The brown rice gives this recipe great texture, but it is the tart yogurt, lemon zest, and fresh fruit that really make me love it. This is the closest thing to a real dessert in this cookbook—though it is only lightly sweetened with honey—but you can just as easily eat it for a decadent breakfast.

This is my mom's original recipe, left untouched by my cheffy impulses. When I was growing up, this was often the way that we used leftover cooked brown rice.

NOTE This rice pudding is at its best with whatever fresh fruit is in season. My favorite is the one below, with fresh peaches, but you can substitute 1 cup of any fresh fruit you like: grated apples, sliced nectarines, or whole blueberries will all work wonderfully.

Unsalted butter, for the baking dish

1 cup **whole milk**

¼ cup **honey**

½ teaspoon ground **cinnamon**

5 grates of **nutmeg**

1 teaspoon **unsweetened vanilla extract**

¼ teaspoon **kosher salt**

2 large **eggs**

2 cups cooked **brown rice**

½ teaspoon grated **lemon zest**

½ cup **raisins**

1 cup diced fresh **peaches** (or whatever fruit you like that is in season) or even frozen peaches

1 cup **whole-milk yogurt**

EQUIPMENT 8-inch square baking dish and an immersion blender (or whisk)

Preheat the oven to 400°F. Butter an 8 × 8-inch baking dish.

In a large bowl, combine the milk, honey, cinnamon, nutmeg, vanilla, salt, and eggs. Using an immersion blender (or whisk), blend it thoroughly until all of the ingredients are fully unified.

Add the rice, lemon zest, raisins, and peaches and stir them thoroughly to combine.

Pour the rice mixture into the baking dish, using a spatula to get any last bits of liquid out of the bowl.

Bake the pudding for 15 minutes. Stir the pudding with a spatula, return to the oven, and bake until the pudding is bubbling around the edges, about 10 minutes longer. If it is not bubbling, increase the temperature to 425°F and bake for an additional 5 minutes.

Remove the pudding from the oven. Add the yogurt and stir just to combine. Let the pudding sit for 5 minutes. This can be enjoyed warm and fresh, or cold out of the fridge (just allow it to cool to room temperature before refrigerating).

healthful snacks

(things that are good for you,
that you will actually want to snack on)

← Rosemary-Tamari Almonds, page 42

Rosemary-Tamari Almonds

Makes 1½ cups

I really love the pairing of rosemary and tamari. They marry into an earthy, umami-rich fragrance that wafts through the kitchen when you roast these almonds. These are the most popular snack in my pantry.

Doubling this recipe is highly encouraged.

2 sprigs fresh **rosemary**, leaves stripped from the stem

1½ cups (8 ounces/225g) raw **almonds**

½ teaspoon **tamari**

1 tablespoon **olive oil**

½ teaspoon **crushed red pepper** or **ichimi** (Japanese red pepper) (optional)

¾ teaspoon **kosher salt**, or more to taste

EQUIPMENT Sheet pan and parchment paper or silicone baking mat

Preheat the oven to 300°F (149°C). Line a sheet pan with parchment paper or a silicone baking mat.

Rub the rosemary leaves together with your fingertips to help open up the oils and their fragrance, then add them to a medium bowl. Add the almonds, tamari, olive oil, crushed red pepper (if using), and salt and toss them together until thoroughly combined.

Pour the nut mixture onto the baking sheet and roast until the nuts are aromatic and have taken on some light color, about 20 minutes, stirring halfway through.

Remove the almonds and let them cool for a minute. Taste for seasoning, adding salt if you desire.

Eat while warm or allow them to cool to room temperature, then store, covered, at room temperature, for up to 1 week.

Coconut-Wakame Trail Mix

Makes about 3 cups

This is a salty riff on trail mix, giving you loads of crispy, crunchy, nutty things, with toasted coconut shreds and crackling seaweed tidbits. It is the perfect thing to pretend you are going to bring on a hike, but in actuality will just keep eating handfuls of every time you walk near your kitchen.

With regard to the seaweed: Nearly any dried seaweed that is used for a seaweed salad will work. Just try to avoid especially thick pieces (like some dashi kombu), or it will be too tough to eat.

If you want to use sheets of roasted nori, you can do so, but it makes for a slightly different process. Use only ½ ounce of nori, and grind it up into a coarse texture with a mortar and pestle before mixing it with the rest of the ingredients.

1 ounce **dried wakame** (or ½ ounce roasted nori sheets)

1½ cups (8 ounces) **raw almonds**

½ cup (3 ounces) **pumpkin seeds**

½ cup (1 ounce) **unsweetened coconut flakes**

4 teaspoons **olive oil**

1 tablespoon **white sesame seeds**

2 teaspoons **tamari**

¼ teaspoon **cayenne pepper**

EQUIPMENT Sheet pan and parchment paper or silicone baking mat

Preheat the oven to 300°F. Line a sheet pan with parchment paper or a silicone baking mat.

In a medium bowl, combine the seaweed, almonds, pumpkin seeds, coconut flakes, olive oil, sesame seeds, tamari, and cayenne and toss them until completely combined. Transfer them to the lined pan.

Roast the trail mix until the coconut has turned a golden brown color and the almonds have darkened slightly, about 20 minutes, stirring it halfway through.

Let the mixture cool on the pan for a minute. Taste for seasoning and add salt if needed. Eat while warm or allow it to cool to room temperature, then store, covered, at room temperature, for up to 1 week.

Olive Oil Kale Chips

Makes 1 tray of chips

These are perhaps my wife's favorite things that I make—which is information that I find quite frustrating, due to the fact that I did not invent them and they are also very easy to prepare. But I get it. They are crispy, satisfying, and nutritious, while containing just three ingredients.

The process is simple: Kale leaves are stripped of their stems and midribs, roughly torn, tossed in olive oil and salt, and then baked at a fairly low heat until they are crispy. If they don't all get eaten straight off the pan throughout the day, they will also stay crispy in a sealed container for 2 to 3 days.

If you find that they are taking longer than you would like to become crispy, I implore you not to raise the heat, or else they might turn slightly bitter.

Any kale works—the curly kind will be crunchier and craggier, while Tuscan kale will have more of a snap. Red kale works wonderfully, too. If you have a wire cooling rack to bake them on, I think it cooks a little more evenly, but it works quite well without it, too.

About 12 **kale leaves**

1 tablespoon **olive oil**

Salt

EQUIPMENT Sheet pan and parchment paper (or a wire cooling rack that fits inside the sheet pan)

Preheat the oven to 275°F. If you have a wire cooling rack, set it inside a sheet pan. Otherwise, line the pan with parchment paper.

Strip the stems and midribs from the leaves and discard them. Roughly tear the kale leaves into pieces that are slightly larger than you want the chips to turn out (sometimes I just leave them as big, whole leaves). Place the leaves in a bowl and add the olive oil, mixing them thoroughly with your hands so that all of the leaves are nicely saturated with oil. Dry leaves will turn bitter. Season them lightly with salt and toss them again.

Arrange them in a single layer on the rack or lined pan, doing your best not to let the leaves overlap.

Roast the leaves until they are crisp all over, occasionally checking the oven and separating any overlapping leaves as they cook. They are usually fully crisp after about 25 minutes.

Remove the kale from the oven and taste one chip for seasoning, sprinkling more salt if needed. Eat them right away or let them cool completely and then transfer them to a sealed container.

Shichimi Popcorn

Serves 2 to 4

My wife describes herself as "the Steph Curry of comedy, because of how much we both love popcorn." This is all to say that after trying many different seasonings on popcorn in our house, shichimi has become her favorite one.

Shichimi, for those unfamiliar with it, is a Japanese spice mixture. The name refers to the number of ingredients (*shichi* meaning "seven" in Japanese), and among other seasonings commonly includes red chile, dried orange peel, seaweed, ground ginger, and sesame. Because it's a salt-free spice mix, you can add as much of it as you please, giving a nutty, spicy (but not too spicy), addictive coating to your popcorn.

This recipe is also an opportunity to rave about how great Ghee (page 18) is for making popcorn, as it adds the flavor of butter without all of the solids that would burn if you tried to pop your popcorn in normal old butter. You can also just use oil (I prefer peanut) and add melted butter after the fact. Or even more simply, you can just microwave popcorn and pour shichimi on it.

NOTE   It's very easy to make your own popcorn salt! It's just really finely ground salt, which helps it to coat the popcorn more easily. I just take kosher salt and grind it with a mortar and pestle, or blitz it in a food processor or coffee grinder.

5 tablespoons **Ghee** (page 18) or 3 tablespoons **oil** (such as peanut, grapeseed, or vegetable)

½ cup **popcorn kernels**

Rounded ½ teaspoon **popcorn salt** (see Note), or to taste

2 teaspoons **shichimi**, plus more to taste

2 to 3 tablespoons **butter**, melted (if you are not using ghee)

EQUIPMENT Large heavy-bottomed pot with a lid (such as a Dutch oven)

In a large heavy-bottomed pot, heat the ghee (or oil) over medium-high heat. Once it is melted (or shimmering, if it is oil), add the popcorn and salt. Cover the pot and shake it frequently. Continue cooking, listening for popping sounds. Once the corn begins to pop, turn the heat down to medium, continuing to shake the pot, briefly and occasionally opening the lid just a crack to let some steam out. Once the popcorn is popping with great frequency, continue shaking the pot until there is a three-second gap with no pops. Remove the pan from the heat and uncover (a kernel or two may try to escape).

Transfer half of the popcorn to a large bowl and season it with half of the shichimi (and melted butter, if you were not using ghee). Add the rest of the popcorn and shichimi (and melted butter, if necessary) and toss it until well combined. Eat it immediately.

Ginger-Habanero Carrot Pickles

Makes one 1-quart jar

While shelf-stable pickling and room-temperature fermentation require science, math, and careful sealing techniques to prevent things like, say, botulism, refrigerator pickles involve a much simpler, easier process.

In this case, you simply boil vinegar, water, and salt, then pour it into a jar packed with carrot sticks, fresh habaneros, sliced ginger, and spices—creating a crunchy, spicy, spiced, and healthful snack that gets spicier the longer it sits in the fridge. I love the bright, fruity heat of habaneros and how they, along with the ginger, do very nice things to a carrot stick. While many fridge pickles call for sugar, I think that carrots don't need any.

The carrot pickles will last about a month in the fridge, if they make it that long before you eat them.

12 ounces (or so) **carrots**

4 **habaneros**

2 ounces fresh **ginger**, washed and sliced into thin coins

1 tablespoon **black mustard seeds** (or any mustard seeds)

½ teaspoon **black peppercorns**

1 cup **distilled white vinegar**

1 cup **water**

¼ teaspoon **fine sea salt**

EQUIPMENT 1-quart mason jar with a lid and a medium saucepan

Thoroughly wash a 1-quart mason jar with hot water (a dishwasher is great for sanitizing a jar). You can also boil it if you want to be certain that your jar is fully sanitized.

Wash the carrots (I don't bother peeling them), then cut off the stems or stem-end and remove any protruding bits of hairy fibers. Slice the carrots into sticks that are about ½ inch thick, then cut down any long ones so that they will fit comfortably in the jar. With the tip of a knife, cut a small "X" into the blossom end (aka not the stem end) of the habaneros and discard the stems.

Place the ginger, habaneros, mustard seeds, and peppercorns in the mason jar. Add the carrot sticks, pushing them in tightly, if necessary, to make sure they all fit.

In a medium saucepan, bring the vinegar, water, and salt to a boil. Remove from the heat and pour the hot liquid directly into the jar. If the carrots are not completely submerged, you can top it off with a little more vinegar until they are covered. Allow the liquid to come to room temperature, then seal the lid and transfer to the fridge.

The pickles can be eaten right away, but are better after 24 hours and at their best starting around day 3.

White Bean Hummus with Lemon, Parsley, and Black Pepper

Makes about 1½ cups

I was throwing a small party at our house when someone arrived whom my wife quickly, quietly, pointed out was vegan. It occurred to me that all of the snacks that we had set out were decidedly not vegan. She privately told my wife not to worry about it, but I worried. So I quickly pulled out my food processor, opened a can of white beans, and made this dip in about 90 seconds.

(The aforementioned person was not, it turns out, hungry after all. But everyone else ate it.)

Additionally, this is a great way to use up any leftover beans from A Pot of Beans (page 2) and works well with most any bean. You may just need to adjust the amount of oil, depending on the starchiness of the bean. I use this as a dip for crudités, bread, crackers, or even as a base for a veggie sandwich or wrap.

1¾ cups cooked **white beans** or 1 (15-ounce) can beans

2 **garlic cloves**, peeled

¼ cup loosely packed fresh **parsley leaves and tender stems**

3 tablespoons fresh **lemon juice**, plus more to taste

¼ cup **olive oil**

½ teaspoon freshly ground **black pepper**, plus more to taste

Salt

EQUIPMENT Sieve and food processor or blender

Drain the beans in a sieve and rinse off any excess starch. Let sit for a minute to allow as much of the water to drain off as possible.

Meanwhile, in a food processor or blender, combine the garlic and parsley and blend it until it comes to a coarsely chopped texture.

Add the drained beans, lemon juice, olive oil, black pepper, and a sprinkling of salt and blend it until it has a smooth texture. If it is a bit dry or grainy, you can add a little more oil. Season it to taste with more salt, black pepper, and lemon juice, as you desire.

It will keep in the refrigerator, covered, for about 1 week.

Jalapeño-Pesto Hummus

Makes about 1½ cups

This is a bit of a riff on the previous White Bean Hummus (page 50), doubling as a way to make use of some leftover pesto. The addition of jalapeño gives it a nice kick.

1¾ cups cooked **white beans** or 1 (15-ounce) can beans

1 **jalapeño, serrano,** or **Fresno chile**, stemmed

¼ cup **Green Vegetable Pesto** (page 114) or **Miso-Spinach Pesto** (page 117)

2 tablespoons fresh **lemon juice**, plus more to taste

2 tablespoons **olive oil**

Salt

EQUIPMENT Sieve and food processor (or blender)

Drain the beans in a sieve and rinse off any excess starch. Let sit for a minute to allow as much of the water to drain off as possible.

Meanwhile, in a food processor or blender, process the chile until it comes to a coarsely chopped texture.

Add the drained beans, pesto, lemon juice, olive oil, and a sprinkling of salt and blend it until it has a smooth texture. If it is a bit dry or grainy, you can add a little more oil. Season it to taste with more salt and lemon juice, as you desire.

It will keep in the refrigerator, covered, for about 1 week.

A CRUDITÉS PARTY

When my wife and I have a party, we love to lay butcher paper down on a table or center kitchen island and then arrange it with colorful farmers market produce, crackers, cheeses, and all of the various dips from this book: Caesar Salad Crudités (page 86), Vegan Tahini Dressing (page 75), White Bean Hummus (page 50), Jalapeño-Pesto Hummus (page 51), and Probiotic Ranch (page 79). The fun (okay, fun to me) part about butcher paper is that you can then label everything right on the paper with a Sharpie—in anyone's handwriting other than mine.

White Bean Hummus

Jalapeño Pesto Hummus

Probiotic Ranch

Tahini Dressing

Caesar

vegetables

(often cooked but sometimes not)

← Purple Tahini Slaw, page 58

Charred Vegetables with Spiced Labneh

Serves 4

This dish was inspired by my friend, the delightfully talented chef Jeremy Fox (I will borrow from him several times in this book, with his generous permission). He had a simple dish of labneh (a thick drained yogurt), spiced with sumac as a dip for raw carrots. I found myself frequently wanting to spice labneh, while never remembering to buy sumac. So I began to spice my labneh—though you can also use Greek yogurt—with chili powder, dried oregano, grated garlic, salt, and black pepper.

It all led to this dish: charred vegetables, still quite hot from the grill (or skillet or broiler), placed directly on top of the spiced labneh, drizzled with olive oil, and topped with grated cheese. The heat wilts the spiced labneh, and it is best enjoyed eaten with your fingers, swiping the vegetables through the tart, spiced condiment beneath. It has been a frequent hit at dinner parties—or most often, my wife and I will just eat it alone while standing at the kitchen counter and deciding what else we should have for dinner, if anything.

NOTE So many vegetables work well for this dish. Snap peas, broccolini, or baby broccoli are quite popular. If you happen to come across sprouting cauliflower at a farmers market, that is probably my favorite version (Thao Family Farm grows my favorite one in the world). But you can also use something as simple as winter grocery store cauliflower florets. The basic idea: You want to char the outside of a vegetable as best you can, while keeping it slightly crunchy at the center, and then plop it directly onto your spiced labneh.

Spiced Labneh

8 ounces **labneh** or **Greek yogurt**

1 **garlic clove**, grated or finely chopped

½ tablespoon **dark chili powder**

⅛ teaspoon **dried oregano**

Freshly ground **black pepper**

Salt

Charred Vegetables

1 pound **vegetable** of your choice (see Note), such as baby broccoli or sugar snap peas

Neutral oil

Salt

Make the spiced labneh: In a bowl, combine the labneh, garlic, chili powder, oregano, black pepper, and salt to taste. Mix them thoroughly, making sure that any corners of labneh have been fully incorporated. Transfer it back to the labneh container (or any sealable container) and let it bloom for at least 30 minutes. It can be kept at room temperature for up to 2 hours, or refrigerated for up to 3 days. If it has been refrigerated, it is best to let it sit out for about 30 minutes before you serve it.

Char the vegetables: Right before you start to char your vegetables, set out a serving platter and spread the labneh across it in a fairly even layer. Set it aside while you cook your vegetables.

In a large bowl, toss the vegetables with a thin, scant layer of neutral oil and season them lightly with salt.

Grill Method Preheat an outdoor grill until it is quite hot. Grill the vegetables until they are blackened a bit on the outside and just barely tender on the inside. If you are grilling smaller pieces, like florets or snap peas, a grill basket is recommended. Once they are cooked, lay them immediately onto the spiced labneh, in a single layer. Some overlapping is not a problem.

Broiler Method Preheat the broiler to high. Line a baking sheet with foil.

Lay the vegetables on the baking sheet in a single layer. Place the baking sheet on the second-highest rack of your oven and broil until they are just blackened, about

To Finish

Olive oil

Freshly grated **hard aged cheese**, such as Parmesan, cheddar, or Gruyère

Salt

EQUIPMENT Grill, broiler (and baking sheet), or heavy skillet

2 minutes. Flip them over and blacken them on the other side—but if they are already cooked to your liking, simply take them out. It is best if the vegetables are not overcooked, even if they don't blacken on both sides. Once they are cooked, lay them immediately onto the spiced labneh, in a single layer. Some overlapping is not a problem.

Skillet Method Place a heavy-bottomed skillet over high heat. Once it is quite hot, add the vegetables in batches, searing them quickly with as much direct contact on the pan as possible, taking care not to crowd them in the pan. Once they have your desired color and are just barely cooked through, transfer them to the labneh in a single layer and repeat with the rest of them.

To finish: Once all of the vegetables are cooked and placed on the spiced labneh, drizzle them liberally with olive oil and top with grated cheese. Season them with salt to taste and eat them immediately.

Purple Tahini Slaw

Serves about 4 as a side

This spicy, nutty, vegan coleslaw is surprisingly universal and delicious, thanks to the vegan tahini dressing. It gets some heat from diced Fresno chiles, but you can also omit them if you are heat sensitive. I love this slaw next to a piece of grilled fish, or the Fillet of Sole (page 159) coated with herbed panko bread crumbs, or as an accompaniment to a deli sandwich, or even next to a grilled bratwurst.

You can keep the coleslaw leftovers, but the salt will slowly begin to leach water from the cabbage, diluting the dressing and taking out some of the crunch. It is best eaten within an hour of dressing. You can, however, make up the salad and just wait to dress it until it is time to serve.

1 small head **red cabbage**

3 tablespoons finely chopped fresh **parsley**

2 medium **carrots**, grated

1 **Fresno** or **jalapeño chile**, seeded and finely chopped (optional)

3 tablespoons **Vegan Tahini Dressing** (page 75), plus more to taste

Salt

Halve the cabbage through the core. Use a knife to cut out the core on each side in a V-shape (discard the core). Cut each half in half again (you have now quartered a head of cabbage!). Lay a quarter down on the cutting board so that it rests securely, then slice it into thin strips. (Alternatively, you can use a mandoline to shred the cabbage on the thinnest setting, being careful, of course, not to shred your fingers.)

In a large bowl, combine the cabbage, parsley, carrots, and chile and toss thoroughly. Add the dressing and mix well. Taste for seasoning and add salt as needed.

Eat immediately, or within an hour or so.

A Roasted Sweet Potato

Makes as many as you want

I tried to get fancy. I played with chopped and roasted sweet potatoes, spiced with shichimi and rice vinegar. I tried roasting them with garlic and tamari and chile de árbol.

But ultimately I discovered what I probably always knew: My favorite way to eat a sweet potato is to roast it whole until the skin is crisp and the inside is soft, and then eat it drizzled with olive oil, sprinkled with salt and pepper, and finished with a squeeze of lemon. Iliza describes it as "Healthy Sour Patch Kids," which I'm fully in favor of, if it convinces people to eat it.

This recipe can, of course, be scaled up very easily—cook as many sweet potatoes as you would like to eat. You can also use this same method (and condiment application) on baked russet potatoes. This is one of the most common side dishes in our house, especially with something like the Fillet of Sole (page 159) or Crispy Roast Chicken with Chile-Scallion Butter (page 172).

1 **sweet potato**

1 teaspoon or so **neutral oil**

Kosher salt

Wedge of **lemon**

Extra-virgin olive oil, for drizzling

Freshly ground **black pepper**

EQUIPMENT Small baking dish and foil or parchment (optional)

Preheat the oven to 425°F. Line a baking dish with foil or parchment. (This is not required, but makes for much easier cleanup, as the sugars in the sweet potato will leak out and caramelize.)

Pierce the sweet potato eight or so times with the tines of a fork. Coat it lightly with the neutral oil and then sprinkle it liberally with salt.

Roast the potato until it is completely tender, usually around 45 minutes, depending on the size of the potato.

Split it open and then finish with a squeeze of lemon, a drizzle of olive oil, more salt, and freshly ground pepper to taste.

Gruyère, Leek, and Swiss Chard Pie

Serves 4 to 6

The combination of leeks, Swiss chard, melted Gruyère, and pie crust is unassailably delicious. This one is another of my mother's creations, with a parbaked crust and a layer of Gruyère cheese on the bottom of the pie, which gets topped with Swiss chard and leeks that have been sautéed in butter. Then the whole thing gets layered with more grated cheese and finished in the oven.

It is a perfect pie when hot from the oven, with leftovers reheating well, too.

½ recipe **Mom's Pie Crust** (page 20)

2 tablespoons **unsalted butter**

2 cups chopped **leeks**, white and light-green parts only (from about 2 large or 3 medium leeks)

2 **garlic cloves**, chopped

Salt

About 18 **Swiss chard** leaves (from 3 to 4 bunches), stems and midribs removed and discarded, leaves washed and roughly chopped

Freshly ground **black pepper**

Flour, for dusting

1½ cups freshly grated **Gruyère cheese** (about 4¼ ounces)

EQUIPMENT Large sauté pan or skillet, rolling pin, 9-inch pie pan, parchment paper, and pie weights (or dried beans)

Make and chill the pie dough as directed.

While the dough is chilling, start the filling. In a large sauté pan, heat the butter over medium heat until melted. Add the leeks and garlic, season them with salt, and sauté, stirring occasionally, until they are translucent, about 10 minutes.

Add the Swiss chard and season it with salt and pepper, then continue sautéing, stirring occasionally, until the chard is cooked down and nicely softened, another 10 minutes. If your pan is too small, you can add the chard a little at a time, adding more as it wilts. Once it is cooked, taste the chard for seasoning and add more as needed. Set it aside until it is time to assemble the pie.

If the dough has been chilling for longer than 1 hour, you may need to let it sit at room temperature until it is less stiff and easier to roll. Transfer the dough to a lightly floured surface. Flour a rolling pin and press down into the center of the dough. Roll the dough out in each direction, starting from the center each time, until you have a round of dough that is ⅛ inch thick, being careful that it is not too thin. Don't worry about any broken bits, rips, or crumbled edges—you can just reattach the dough.

Lay the dough over a 9-inch pie pan, making sure it is flat against the entire surface. Cut off any excess dough, leaving about an inch of overhanging dough, and then fold it under itself. If there are any rips or holes, you can patch them with the extra dough. Use your thumb and forefinger to fold and crimp the edges of the pie dough—or you can use the tines of a fork to press against the edges of the crust, all the way around.

Use a fork to stab the bottom and sides of the pie shell several times. Place the pie shell in the refrigerator for at least 30 minutes to help it set. Meanwhile, preheat the oven to 425°F.

Once the oven is preheated and the pie shell is chilled, lay a piece of parchment over the crust and fill it with pie weights or dried beans. Bake until the crust is just barely set and cooked, about 15 minutes. Remove from the oven, but leave the oven on.

Remove the parchment and pie weights. Sprinkle half of the cheese over the bottom of the pie crust, then top with the chard mixture in an even layer. Top it with the rest of the cheese.

Return to the oven and bake until the cheese is melted and the crust is golden brown, about 20 minutes.

Allow the pie to cool briefly, then cut and serve.

Kevin Bludso's Mama's Spinach Pie

Serves 6 to 8

Kevin Bludso is one of the most acclaimed pitmasters in the world, a food television star, the owner and creator of Bludso's Bar & Que, and as luck would have it, a mentor, big brother, and very close friend of mine. My smoked potato breakfast burrito recipe found its way to the pages of his cookbook, and he was kind enough to offer up this spinach pie for mine. Though as it turns out, this recipe is much more of something that his mother makes, so he sent me off to talk to her for the details. When I asked her how she would like to be credited, she said: "Kevin's mama. I don't care about any credit."

This pie actually reminds me somewhat of a spinach casserole: Croutons line the bottom of a baking dish, which is then topped with a mixture of blanched spinach, crumbled bacon, cubes of cheddar cheese, butter, eggs, and cottage cheese, which gets baked off in the oven. It should come as no surprise to anyone that it is absolutely delicious.

I reduced the amount of bacon slightly from what Kevin's mother typically uses—but by all means feel free to increase those quantities to your taste. You could also omit the bacon altogether and it would be delicious, too.

About 4 cups **Cheddar Croutons** (page 87) or an herbed crouton—enough to line the bottom of the baking dish in a single layer

About 1½ pounds **spinach leaves**

8 ounces **cheddar cheese**, cut into ½-inch or so cubes

1 pound **cottage cheese**

3 large **eggs**, lightly beaten

3 tablespoons **unsalted butter**, melted

4 slices **bacon**, cooked until crisp

Salt and freshly ground **black pepper**

EQUIPMENT A large pot for blanching spinach, 9 × 13-inch baking dish, and a large sieve

Preheat the oven to 375°F.

Bring a large pot of water to a boil. Meanwhile, line the bottom of a 9 × 13-inch baking dish with a single layer of the croutons.

Once the water is boiling, add the spinach leaves to it and give them a stir. Allow them to just barely wilt—this will take about 10 seconds—then transfer them to a sieve and rinse them under cold water. Once they are cool enough to handle, squeeze out as much liquid as you can with your hands. Transfer the spinach to a cutting board and give it a rough chop.

Add the spinach to a large bowl along with the cheddar, cottage cheese, eggs, and melted butter. Use your hands to crumble the bacon into the bowl and stir the mixture until it is well combined. Season it with salt and pepper, keeping in mind that the bacon already has a lot of salt to it.

Lay the spinach mixture over the croutons in an even layer. Transfer the dish to the oven and bake until it is just set and the cheese is melted, about 30 minutes. If you would like a little more color, you can finish it under the broiler for an extra minute or two.

The spinach pie can be served right away. I also find that it reheats very well.

Barbara's Potato and Squash Gratin

Serves 6 to 8

In Paso Robles, California, there was a peaceful oasis of a place called Windrose Farm. It was owned by Bill and Barbara Spencer—two of the warmest, kindest, and most thoughtful people I have ever met in my life—before they recently sold the farm. I got to know them briefly some years ago at the Santa Monica Farmers Market and had the pleasure of staying a night on their farm once when I was driving up north. Their fifty-acre farm is forever a calming memory for me, filled with apple trees, lambs, shishito peppers, and even a large vertical smoker that smells intoxicatingly of their own apple wood, where they smoke things like garlic bulbs, tomatoes, and meat.

Several years ago, when I saw her at the farmers market, Barbara told me that I should make a gratin using her squash and some Swiss chard from the table across from hers. She talked me through the recipe and it has graced my Thanksgiving table every year since, evolving and changing from time to time based on what I had on hand and what I remembered. I hope this version does it justice.

Olive oil

1 large bunch **Swiss chard**

1 large (or 2 medium) **leeks**, white and light-green parts only

6 **garlic cloves**, peeled

Salt and freshly ground **black pepper**

1 medium **butternut squash** (about 3 pounds)

1 pound waxy **yellow potatoes**

2½ cups grated **melting cheese**, such as Gruyère

EQUIPMENT
3-quart baking dish

Preheat the oven to 350°F. Grease a shallow 3-quart baking dish with olive oil.

Remove the stems and midribs from the chard and set the leaves aside. Finely chop the leeks, garlic, and chard stems together. Sprinkle the mixture across the bottom of the baking dish. Drizzle them with a little more olive oil and season them with salt and a few twists of freshly ground black pepper.

Peel the squash and quarter it lengthwise, discarding the strings and seeds. Cut each quarter crosswise into ¼-inch-thick slices. Slice the potatoes into ¼-inch-thick slices. Place the squash and potatoes in a bowl and toss them with 1½ tablespoons olive oil and season them with salt and pepper—you can be fairly liberal with the salt, as it will be salting the chard as well.

To assemble the gratin, arrange a layer of chard leaves on the bottom, followed by a layer of squash and then potatoes—repeating until you have used everything up. Don't worry if it looks rustic and has bits of chard sticking out, or a scant quantity of potatoes and squash for the final layer—it simply adds to the charm.

Cover the gratin with foil, transfer to the oven, and bake for 30 minutes. Remove the foil and bake it until the potatoes and squash are cooked through and the top layer of the gratin has begun to take on some color, another hour or so.

Top the gratin with the grated cheese and return it to the oven, allowing it to cook until the cheese has melted. If you would like your cheese to be a bit browned, you can finish it under the broiler—but there is something really nice about soft, gooey melted cheese.

Remove the gratin from the oven and allow it to cool slightly before serving.

Broccoli-Sausage Bread

Serves 4

Most people would probably call this a stromboli, but when I was growing up, I only knew it as Broccoli Bread. While you can make a vegetarian version with sautéed broccoli only, I think that the extra fat from the sausage really turns it into something special. Broccoli and sausage, whether in pasta form (page 102) or here, is one of my all-time favorite flavor combinations. Iliza swears that it wants marinara sauce to dip into, but I politely disagree.

As a kid, I used to get excited about any leftover broccoli bread and would eat it cold out of the fridge the next day.

If you're making homemade pizza dough from scratch for this, I recommend making the dough first and then preparing the filling while the dough proofs. But of course, if you are short on time, you can also buy pizza dough and use that here instead of homemade.

I usually use a full batch of Nearly Pizza Dough, divided in half, and then make 2 breads. To do that, simply double the recipe and bake both Broccoli-Sausage Breads at the same time (or one Broccoli-Sausage and one Krauty Smoked Cheddar Broccoli Bread).

A halved batch of **Nearly Pizza Dough** (page 21) (about 9 ounces) or half of a 1-pound ball of store-bought pizza dough

1 tablespoon **olive oil**

8 ounces **Cal-Italian Pork Sausage with Rosemary and Orange Zest** (page 15) or store-bought sweet Italian sausage (casings removed)

2 **garlic cloves**, chopped

3 cups finely chopped **broccoli florets** (from about 2 stalks)

Salt and freshly ground **black pepper**

½ teaspoon **dried oregano**

Pinch of **crushed red pepper**

Flour, for rolling out

1 **egg** (optional)

EQUIPMENT Skillet, baking sheet, parchment paper, rolling pin or wine bottle, and a pastry brush (optional)

If the dough (either homemade or store-bought) was refrigerated, set it out for 30 minutes to 1 hour to come to room temperature.

Meanwhile, in a skillet, heat the oil over medium heat until shimmering. Add the sausage and fry it until it is just beginning to brown around the edges, breaking it up with a cooking spoon to help it crumble while it cooks, about 7 minutes.

Add the garlic and stir it together with the sausage, then add the broccoli and season it with salt and pepper. Add the oregano and crushed red pepper and stir to combine. Add a splash of water and deglaze the pan, scraping up any browned sausage bits and stirring them in. Continue cooking, stirring occasionally, until the sausage is cooked through and the broccoli is tender but still has a tiny bit of bite left to it, 8 to 10 minutes. Remove from the heat and set aside.

Preheat the oven to 375°F. Line a baking sheet with parchment paper.

When your dough is ready, lightly flour a work surface and place the dough on it. Lightly flour a rolling pin and roll the dough into a thin rectangle about 16 × 9 inches. Don't worry too much about it being pretty or perfect. It can be quite rustic. Shake the dough lightly and lift it, making sure it is not stuck to the surface.

Lay the broccoli/sausage filling across the dough, leaving about 1 inch of space around the outer edges. With a long side facing you, roll up the dough like a jelly-roll, pressing down gently as you roll. Prepare to lift it up with both hands—you can even tug it a bit here, to extend its length just slightly—and place it, seam-side down, on the lined baking sheet. It should be a fairly sturdy dough. If you are baking a second bread, make sure to leave room on the baking sheet.

Use a knife to make four shallow cuts along the top, like on a baguette. →

← Crack an egg into a bowl and whisk it with a tablespoon or so of water. Use a pastry brush to paint an egg wash along the top of the bread. You can omit this step if you would like, but I prefer the glossier color the crust gets from the egg wash.

Bake until the exterior is golden brown and the dough inside is cooked through, about 30 minutes. Allow it to rest at least 10 minutes before cutting it into slices. Serve it either hot or at room temperature.

Krauty Smoked Cheddar Broccoli Bread

Serves 4

I was playing with various vegetarian versions of the Broccoli-Sausage Bread (page 64) and stumbled into this one, and I have to say I can't get over how much I like it. The smoked cheddar gives a slightly carnivorous nod, but the sauerkraut inside and a dip of mustard brings it all together, somehow combining the Italian-American comfort food and Jewish deli sandwiches of my childhood into a warm swaddling of edible joy and nostalgia.

I usually use a full batch of Nearly Pizza Dough, divided in half, and then make 2 breads. To do that, simply double the recipe and bake both breads at the same time (or one Broccoli-Sausage and one Krauty Smoked Cheddar Broccoli Bread).

A halved batch of **Nearly Pizza Dough** (page 21) (about 9 ounces) or half of a 1-pound ball of store-bought pizza dough

2 tablespoons **olive oil**

3 **garlic cloves**, chopped

3 cups finely chopped **broccoli florets** (from about 2 stalks)

Salt and freshly ground **black pepper**

½ teaspoon **dried oregano**

Pinch of **crushed red pepper**

Flour, for rolling out

4 ounces **smoked cheddar cheese**, cut into ½-inch cubes

½ cup drained **sauerkraut**

1 **egg** (optional)

2 teaspoons or so of **sesame seeds**

Yellow or deli **mustard**, for serving

EQUIPMENT Skillet, baking sheet, parchment paper, rolling pin or wine bottle, and a pastry brush (optional)

If the dough (either homemade or store-bought) was refrigerated, set it out for 30 minutes to 1 hour to come to room temperature.

Meanwhile, in a skillet heat the oil over medium heat until shimmering. Add the garlic and fry it until it is just beginning to brown around the edges. Add the broccoli and season it with salt and pepper. Add the oregano and crushed red pepper and stir it to combine. Continue cooking, stirring occasionally, until the broccoli is tender but still has a tiny bit of bite left to it, about 10 minutes. If the pan is drying out too much add a small splash of water to help steam the broccoli and finish the cooking—just make sure the water is fully evaporated. Remove from the heat and set aside.

Preheat the oven to 375°F. Line a baking sheet with parchment paper.

When your dough is ready, lightly flour a work surface and place the dough on it. Lightly flour a rolling pin and roll the dough into a long thin rectangle about 16 × 9 inches. Don't worry too much about it being pretty or perfect. It can be quite rustic. Shake the dough lightly and lift it, making sure it is not stuck to the surface.

Lay the filling across the dough, leaving about 1 inch of space around the outer edge. Scatter the smoked cheddar over the filling, followed by the sauerkraut. With a long side facing you, roll up the dough like a jelly-roll, pressing down gently as you roll it. Prepare to lift it up with both hands—you can even tug it a bit here, to extend its length just slightly—and then place it, seam-side down, on the lined baking sheet. It should be a fairly sturdy bread. If you are baking a second bread, make sure to leave room on the baking sheet.

Use a knife to make four shallow cuts along the top, like on a baguette.

Crack an egg into a bowl and whisk it with a tablespoon or so of water. Use a pastry brush to paint an egg wash along the top. You can omit this step if you would like, but I prefer the glossier color the crust gets from the egg wash. Top the egg wash with a sprinkling of the sesame seeds. (If you are avoiding the egg wash and still want the sesame seeds, you can brush the bread with water instead to help the seeds to adhere.)

Bake until the exterior is golden brown and the dough inside is cooked through, about 30 minutes. Allow it to rest at least 10 minutes before cutting it into slices. Serve it, either hot or at room temperature, with a side of mustard for dipping.

Hippie California New Year's Dinner

(or, three sides as a meal)

In the South, there is a long tradition of eating cornbread, greens, and black-eyed peas on New Year's Day. When my mom (an Italian-American from upstate New York) was living in Miami, she learned of this tradition through the cooking of a woman named Fanny Cummings.

There was an iconic rental home in Golden Beach, Florida, where musicians and producers would stay while recording music at Criteria Studios. When, say, The BeeGees or Eric Clapton were making some of their famous records, they would rent out and live at 461 Ocean Boulevard. My dad, Albhy Galuten, was a record producer and musician who was hanging out and playing on records back then (if you look at the album art for Eric Clapton's *461 Ocean Boulevard*, you can see a photo of him climbing a coconut tree). Fanny Cummings cooked for and maintained that beloved house—or as my dad described it, "She made it feel like a home." Maurice Gibb, meanwhile, had never heard the name "Fanny" before, and it became the inspiration for the BeeGees song "Fanny (Be Tender with My Love)."

Thanks to Fanny, the Southern tradition continued in my house growing up. My parents were hippie vegetarians back in the '70s and early '80s, so the idea evolved, but stayed vegetarian while also incorporating some of my mom's Italian flare.

Technically, these are three side dishes, but eaten all together they make one of my favorite meals in the world, each one heightened by the presence of the others. Leftovers reheat well, often turning into a wonderful, sludgy porridge all broken up and combined in a bowl. →

Fresno Chile and White Cheddar Cornbread

Serves 4 to 6

This is a cornbread that veers a little more into a cake-like texture than some of the classic Southern cornbread you might be accustomed to. But it is soft and tender with a nice crust and lots of flavor.

Butter, for the pie pan

1¼ cups (175g) **all-purpose flour**

¾ cup (130g) **cornmeal**

1 tablespoon plus 2 teaspoons (25g) **baking powder**

1 ever-so-slightly heaped teaspoon (7g) **fine sea salt**

1 large **egg**, beaten

1 cup (250g) **buttermilk**

¼ cup (85g) **honey** or (50g) **granulated sugar**

2 tablespoons **unsalted butter**, melted

½ cup fresh **corn kernels** (optional)

1 **Fresno** or **jalapeño chile**, seeded and finely chopped

2 tablespoons finely chopped fresh **parsley**

8 ounces **white cheddar cheese**, freshly grated

EQUIPMENT 9-inch pie pan or cast-iron skillet

Preheat the oven to 375°F. Grease a 9-inch pie pan or cast-iron skillet generously with butter.

In a large bowl, combine the flour, cornmeal, baking powder, and salt. Whisk it thoroughly until it is well combined. Add the egg, buttermilk, honey, melted butter, corn (if using), chile, parsley, and half of the cheddar. Fold the ingredients together until you have a unified, well-mixed batter. It will be somewhat stiff, but that is okay.

Pour the mixture into the pie pan and use a spoon or silicone spatula to even it out a bit. Top it with the remaining grated cheddar.

Bake the cornbread until a cake tester or toothpick inserted into the center comes out clean and the top is golden brown, 25 to 30 minutes. If the inside is done but you want the top more browned, you can quickly finish it under the broiler.

Remove the cornbread from the oven and allow it to rest for at least 15 minutes before cutting and serving.

Vegan Cal-Italian Black-Eyed Peas

Serves 4 to 6

Black-eyed peas are remarkable in the way that they have so many of the properties of a bean, yet taste so distinctly vegetal at the same time (they are technically legumes, as are beans, but are part of the cowpea subspecies). I love Kevin Bludso's version, cooked in a broth of smoked ham hocks and turkey necks, but this version is the one that I grew up eating, and to me it is truly, deeply comforting.

2 tablespoons **olive oil**

½ **onion**, diced (about 1 cup)

½ **green bell pepper**, diced (about 1 cup)

3 **garlic cloves**, chopped

Salt and freshly ground **black pepper**

¾ cup diced **tomato**

3½ cups cooked **black-eyed peas**, with their cooking liquid, or 2 (16-ounce) cans black-eyed peas, undrained

2 teaspoons **balsamic vinegar**

1 teaspoon **tamari**

EQUIPMENT Large skillet

In a large skillet, heat the olive oil over medium heat until it shimmers. Add the onion, bell pepper, and garlic. Season it with salt and black pepper and allow the vegetables to sauté, stirring occasionally, until they are wilted, about 5 minutes.

Add the tomatoes, black-eyed peas, vinegar, and tamari and season with more salt and black pepper and stir together. Increase the heat to medium-high and bring to a high simmer. Reduce the heat to a gentle simmer and cook, stirring the pan occasionally, until the liquid has thickened and reduced to the point that you can drag your spoon across the skillet and the liquid will take a moment before rushing in and filling the empty space.

Taste the peas for seasoning and adjust it as needed. Eat it immediately or keep it warm.

Sautéed Swiss Chard

Serves 4 to 6

These are exceedingly simple greens, sautéed with just olive oil, salt, and some garlic or perhaps a leek. They are simple by design, meant to complement the much more flavorful black-eyed peas and cornbread.

3 tablespoons **olive oil**

4 **garlic cloves**, chopped, or 1 large leek, white and light-green parts only, chopped

2 pounds **Swiss chard**, stems discarded and leaves washed and roughly torn (any water from washing can still be clinging to the leaves)

Salt

EQUIPMENT Large skillet with a lid

In a large skillet, heat the oil over medium-high heat until shimmering. Add the garlic or leek and sauté until just lightly browned at the edges. Add the chard and a sprinkling of salt. Sauté, stirring regularly, for about 1 minute. Reduce the heat to medium, cover, and steam until the chard is quite wilted, about 2 minutes. Uncover and continue cooking until the leaves are tender, about 3 minutes longer. Season to taste with salt and serve.

salads and dressings

(raw things, and the dressings
to coat them with)

← Turmeric Tomato Salad with Fried Herbs and Kitchari Spices, page 88

NO RECIPE LEMON-TAMARI DRESSING

While I love all of the dressings in this book, this is what I often make when I just want to throw a handful of greens in a bowl and have something healthful and quick while talking on the phone or racing between meetings.

Place a handful or two of mixed greens or torn lettuces in a bowl. If I am lucky I have some sliced hearts of palm to toss in, and maybe a few slices of cucumber or the end of a refrigerator-avocado. If I have some sprouts, those may go in, too.

I drizzle some extra-virgin olive oil over it, I squeeze half a lemon on top (usually failing to catch all of the lemon seeds with my other hand), give it a splash of tamari, then season it with flaky salt and freshly ground black pepper. Then I taste it and adjust it (sometimes by adding more lettuce because I made too much dressing). If my wife is having some, I usually grate some Parmesan cheese on top.

Vegan Tahini Dressing

This is one of those recipes that is so simple you might think you need to add something else. You do not. It was created out of a desire for a vegan coleslaw—and it turned into the Purple Tahini Slaw (page 58). But then I liked it so much that it became my favorite dressing for The Hippie California (page 81), and then I just wound up dipping cucumbers into it, which led to me tossing it with soba noodles for the Cold Sesame Soba (page 119).

As a result, this dressing has become a staple in my home—a delightful addition to a salad that comes together in about 30 seconds, and also works as a dip for a crudités board (snap peas are especially good with this). The dressing will look broken as you first start stirring, but after sitting for just a few seconds longer, it hydrates and thickens into something smooth, silky, and alluring.

A note: If it is an especially dry brand of tahini, you may need to increase the olive oil slightly to thin it, and then season it with a bit more salt to compensate as well.

2 tablespoons **tahini**

2 tablespoons **extra-virgin olive oil**

2 teaspoons **rice vinegar**

2 teaspoons **red wine vinegar**

2 teaspoons **tamari**

Salt (optional)

EQUIPMENT Whisk (or fork)

In a small bowl, combine the tahini, olive oil, rice vinegar, wine vinegar, and tamari and whisk them vigorously. Taste for seasoning and add salt if needed. Use the dressing immediately or store in the refrigerator for a few days.

Ginger-Sesame Dressing

Makes about ¾ cup

I tried multiple versions of this dressing—some of them involved sautéing ginger and garlic in sesame oil—before coming to the (now obvious) conclusion that simpler is better. This has become another multiuse dressing that is good for basic side salads. But since it has a lot of acid and no sugar, it is perfect with a salad like the Ginger-Cilantro Chicken Salad (page 85), which gets its sweetness from grated apple and fresh citrus segments.

1½ tablespoons **sesame seeds**, freshly toasted or purchased already roasted

1½ teaspoons finely grated fresh **ginger**

3 tablespoons fresh **lime juice**

3 tablespoons **sesame oil**

3 tablespoons **olive oil**

2 tablespoons **rice vinegar**

1 tablespoon **tamari**

Salt (optional)

EQUIPMENT Grater (for the ginger) and a whisk (or fork)

In a small bowl, combine the sesame seeds, ginger, lime juice, sesame oil, olive oil, vinegar, and tamari and whisk them vigorously. Taste for seasoning and add salt if needed. Use the dressing immediately or store in the refrigerator for a few days.

Shallot Vinaigrette

Makes about 1½ cups

This is probably my favorite vinaigrette for some light, leafy greens to serve alongside a piece of fish or an omelet. The most difficult part of this dressing is the requirement that you mince a shallot—though I'm confident you will be okay. You can also swap it out for any regular onion if you wish, though the vinaigrette will be a little harsher (shallots tend to be a little more subtle).

I frequently make this in a mason jar, keeping leftovers in the fridge for a couple of days, and then use it for small salads when I want one. Try to eat this within 3 days of making it, because the shallot can turn a bit acrid.

NOTE Any mustard will do. I prefer Dijon, which my wife insists she does not like.

¾ cup **extra-virgin olive oil**

¼ cup **red wine vinegar**

1 tablespoon minced **shallot**

2 teaspoons **mustard** (see Note)

¼ teaspoon freshly ground **black pepper**

Salt

EQUIPMENT 1-pint mason jar (ideally with a plastic screw-top)

In a 1-pint mason jar (or other resealable container), combine the oil, vinegar, shallot, mustard, black pepper, and salt to taste. Screw on the lid and shake vigorously for a few seconds until you have a semiunified vinaigrette. Taste for seasoning and adjust it as you desire. Use right away, or store for 3 days under refrigeration. Just make sure to give it a quick shake before you dress your salad.

Chopped Salad Vinaigrette

Makes about ¾ cup

While most classic vinaigrettes have a 3:1 ratio of fat to acid, I believe that a chopped salad should be 1:1. This one uses lemon juice, red wine vinegar, raw garlic, and Dijon mustard, balanced out with just a touch of honey to make a punchy salad dressing that pairs perfectly with the Veggie-Loaded Chop (page 82), but works well on any of the more classic pizzeria chopped salad iterations out there. My wife loves this dressing and does not know that it has Dijon mustard in it.

¼ cup **extra-virgin olive oil**

2 tablespoons fresh **lemon juice**

2 tablespoons **red wine vinegar**

1 small **garlic clove**, grated

½ teaspoon **Dijon mustard**

½ teaspoon **dried oregano**

¼ teaspoon (or a few twists) freshly ground **black pepper**

¼ teaspoon (or just a light drizzle) **honey**

Salt

EQUIPMENT Grater (for the garlic) and a whisk

In a small bowl, combine the oil, lemon juice, vinegar, garlic, mustard, oregano, black pepper, and honey. Add a three-finger pinch of salt and whisk everything together vigorously, making sure that the honey is not clumped at the bottom of the bowl. Taste the dressing for seasoning and add more salt if needed.

It is best right away, but can also be stored in the refrigerator, covered, for up to 3 days. Just make sure to whisk it thoroughly again before adding it to a salad.

Probiotic Ranch

Makes about ⅔ cup

This is a bright, healthful salad dressing that is spiked with all the flavors of ranch dressing but without any mayonnaise, sour cream, buttermilk, or sugar. It is made with probiotic yogurt, livened up with both dried and fresh ingredients. Depending on the brand of yogurt you use, the thickness of this dressing will vary. Sidenote: Doesn't "Probiotic Ranch" sound *way* more appetizing than "Yogurt Vinaigrette"?

I use this dressing with the "Chef Salad" (page 87), but it also works quite well as a dip for crudités.

NOTE I prefer using regular plain yogurt. I avoid using Greek yogurt, as the by-product of the draining that gives Greek yogurt its texture is, in large quantities, toxic for the environment.

½ cup **probiotic plain yogurt**

2 tablespoons **extra-virgin olive oil**

1 tablespoon finely chopped fresh **parsley**

1 **garlic clove**, grated

1 teaspoon fresh **lemon juice**

¼ teaspoon **dried herbs**, such as oregano or Italian seasoning

¼ teaspoon granulated **garlic**

¼ teaspoon granulated **onion**

⅛ teaspoon freshly ground **black pepper**, or more to taste

Salt

EQUIPMENT Grater (for the garlic) and a whisk

In a small bowl, combine the yogurt, oil, parsley, grated garlic, lemon juice, herbs, granulated garlic, granulated onion, and black pepper and whisk to combine. Season to taste with salt. The dressing can be used right away, but the flavor of the dried ingredients will intensify after it has sat for a bit. This dressing will keep for about 5 days in the refrigerator.

The Hippie California

Makes 2 big salads or 4 to 6 side salads

This is my version of the "health food restaurant" salads I enjoyed for most of my life—a nutty vegan dressing with the required dose of crunchy seed things, sprouts, legumes, lettuces, vegetables, and, since it is California, some avocado and citrus. Any lettuce will work, but I'm partial to red leaf lettuce, washed, dried, and roughly torn into big floppy leaves.

You can use any dressing in the book with this salad, but I suggest the Vegan Tahini Dressing (page 75).

NOTE You can use a peeled and segmented orange instead of a tangerine. Simply cut the segments in half, crosswise.

1 head **lettuce** or about 4 cups loosely packed leaves

3 ounces **sprouts**, such as alfalfa, broccoli, daikon, or onion

8 ounces **cucumber** (any type will work), cut into bite-size pieces

1 medium **carrot**, grated

1 cup cooked or canned **chickpeas** (or your bean of choice), drained and rinsed

2 small or 1 medium seedless **tangerine**, divided into segments (see Note)

Vegan Tahini Dressing (page 75)

Salt and freshly ground **black pepper**

1 medium **avocado**

2 tablespoons **sunflower seeds** or **pumpkin seeds**, freshly toasted or purchased already roasted

If you are starting with a head of lettuce, tear it into large rough pieces and then wash and thoroughly dry the leaves. Add them to a large bowl, followed by the sprouts. Break up the sprouts in the bowl a bit and try to disperse them into the lettuce without too much clumping. Add the cucumber, carrot, chickpeas, and tangerine to the bowl. Add the dressing and toss it thoroughly to combine the salad, being careful again of large sprout clumps. Taste the salad for seasoning and then adjust it with salt and freshly ground black pepper.

Divide the salad into individual bowls or one large serving bowl. Halve and pit the avocado, then use a spoon to carve out thin little slices and lay them on top of the salad(s). Season the avocado with a sprinkling of salt. Top the salad(s) with a relatively even coating of sunflower seeds. Serve immediately.

TOASTED CHICKPEA SNACK

If you have some extra chickpeas on hand (like the remnants from the above recipe) and don't want to waste them, dry them off with a towel and then toast them in a skillet over medium heat with a drizzle of olive oil (just enough to coat). Once they are crispy, toss them with some salt, black pepper, and a pinch of turmeric.

Eat them immediately, or allow them to sit out uncovered for up to a few hours. (If you cover them, they will get a little soggy and mushy.)

Veggie-Loaded Chop

*Makes 2 big salads
or 4 to 6 side salads*

This is all about learning how to riff on a chopped salad, using all the ends and bits of loose vegetables that have been hiding in the deepest corners of your fridge. My favorite versions involve a few green beans, a bell pepper, a couple of stalks of celery, a can of beans (or the final remnants of your Pot of Beans [page 2]), some pickled chiles, and aged white cheddar.

Certain vegetables get chopped, blanched in boiling water, and then shocked in ice water. Others just get chopped up raw. But then the whole thing comes together thanks to the Chopped Salad Vinaigrette (page 78) and some sharp cheese. Sadly, I have not yet found a solution for making a chopped salad without chopping a lot of vegetables—and I do think that a small chop (use the size of your canned beans as a guide) is best.

Feel free to riff and modify as you see fit. I find that the most irreplaceable ingredients are the peppery, earthy chopped parsley and crunchy diced celery. But if you, say, happen to have leftover grilled vegetables, you could use those instead of the blanched ones. Or if you would prefer mozzarella or Parmesan to aged white cheddar, be my guest.

Additionally, if you make too much chopped salad mix, it all keeps well in the fridge (undressed) for a few days, so you have a quick salad on hand whenever you need one.

....

Salt

1 cup or so assorted diced **vegetables**, such as asparagus, zucchini, broccolini, green beans, baby broccoli, potatoes, cauliflower, and the like

4 cups diced **lettuces** (I love a combination of romaine, radicchio, and arugula) taking care to not use too much of a bitter lettuce like radicchio or endive

2 **celery stalks**, diced

¼ cup finely chopped fresh **flat-leaf parsley**

½ cup chopped **orange or red bell pepper** (or any raw vegetable you like, such as cucumber, snap peas, or the like)

1¾ cups cooked **beans**, homemade (page 2), or 1 (15-ounce) can, drained and rinsed

Bring a 4-quart or so pot of water to a boil. Meanwhile, fill a large bowl with ice and cold water—this will shock the vegetables after they have been blanched, stopping the cooking process and preserving their bright color.

Once the water is boiling, season it aggressively with salt (it should be briny, like the sea). Add the diced vegetables that you like and have on hand, timing them out according to their cook time so that you can drain them all at the same time. Here is a quick guide to the rough cooking times:

Potato: 5 minutes
Asparagus, baby broccoli, broccolini, cauliflower, green beans: 90 seconds
Zucchini: 50 seconds

Once you've cooked the vegetables, immediately transfer them to the ice bath to shock them, stirring them around with your hand or a spoon. Leave the vegetables in the ice bath for about 5 minutes. After that, you will find that the ice has mostly melted and floated to the top. Scoop the ice out and drain the vegetables well in a sieve. They should be cold, crisp, lightly cooked, and still have a little bit of bite left to them.

In a large bowl, combine the drained vegetables, lettuces, celery, parsley, bell pepper, beans, pickled peppers (if using), and any additional vegetables. Add the vinaigrette and toss gently. Taste it for salt, adding more if needed, while keeping in mind that the cheese is salty.

Divide the salad into bowls and top with grated cheese.

2 tablespoons or so diced **pickled peppers**, such as jalapeños or pepperoncini (optional)

Chopped Salad Vinaigrette (page 78)

Salt

2 ounces **aged white cheddar cheese** (or any cheese that you have on hand), grated with the medium holes of a box grater (about ¾ cup)

EQUIPMENT 4-quart pot for blanching vegetables and a sieve or colander

Ginger-Cilantro Chicken Salad

Makes 2 main-dish salads

Americans love ordering Chinese chicken salad, despite it being an entirely American invention with no roots in China that I am aware of. I suppose I am no different. Since 1981 there has been a restaurant on the Westside of L.A. called Feast from the East, famed for their version. It has been something of the gold standard for that salad for as long as I remember—romaine lettuce, shredded chicken, a sweet-acidic sesame dressing, and crispy wonton strips.

During the pandemic, I was craving this salad—or something resembling it—and along the way started filtering it through my own ideals of what I want from a salad. The result is this: romaine lettuces, shredded cabbage, and pulled leftover chicken, all tossed in a bright ginger/fresh citrus/sesame dressing. Instead of sugar, the dressing gets its sweetness from some grated apple and fresh mandarins. Then, to literally top it all off, it gets a healthy dusting of sizzling, crispy, sliced almonds, toasted in sesame oil and a bit of shichimi.

It is, admittedly, quite far from the Feast from the East version, and even farther away from anything remotely Chinese—but it is delicious, and actually quite healthful, too.

2½ cups chopped **romaine lettuce** (bite-size pieces, about 1 small head)

½ medium head **red cabbage**, finely shredded or thinly sliced

2 cups pulled **chicken** (about 1 large breast, or 2 thighs), fridge-cold

¼ cup tightly packed chopped fresh **cilantro leaves**

1 **apple**, cored and coarsely grated

1 **carrot**, coarsely grated

1 seedless **mandarin** or **tangerine**, peeled and pulled into segments

½ cup sliced **almonds**

Ginger-Sesame Dressing (page 76), used to taste

1 tablespoon **sesame oil**

¼ teaspoon **salt**

1 teaspoon **shichimi**, or to taste

EQUIPMENT Grater and a skillet

In a large bowl, combine the lettuce, cabbage, chicken, cilantro, apple, carrot, and mandarin and toss them together until they are mostly mixed.

Place a skillet over medium heat and add the almonds to it to dry-toast, stirring occasionally.

Meanwhile, add the dressing to the salad and toss thoroughly until everything is fully coated in dressing. Portion the salad into two bowls (or into one big serving bowl, if you'd like) and set them aside while you check on the almonds.

Once the almonds are beginning to become fragrant and brown a bit at the edges (this will take 3 to 4 minutes), add the sesame oil and salt to the skillet and stir constantly. If the oil or the almonds begin to smell bitter or are turning black, reduce the heat. Once you have partial browning—about 1 to 2 minutes—sprinkle in the shichimi and continue stirring for 30 more seconds.

Immediately coat the top of the salad with the hot almond mixture—it might sizzle a little as it lands—and serve right away.

Caesar Salad Crudités

Makes about 1⅓ cups dip

A great Caesar salad is a perfect creation—I like mine with rather a lot of lemon and black pepper—but it does tend to require things like forks and plates. Due to that unfortunate reality, I found myself putting Caesar dressing out at parties as a dip, along with whole leaves of romaine lettuce. It became an instant hit, and is frequently the first thing that needs refreshing.

If you are a person who does not like anchovies, I would tell you to keep them in the dressing anyway. But you can take them out if you would like. This recipe also calls for raw egg yolk, which can potentially cause foodborne illness. Consume raw egg yolk at your own risk.

2 **egg yolks**

4 **anchovy fillets**, roughly chopped (optional)

3 **garlic cloves**, roughly chopped

½ cup grated **Parmigiano-Reggiano cheese**, plus more to taste

¼ cup fresh **lemon juice**, plus more to taste

¼ teaspoon **Dijon mustard**

½ teaspoon **Worcestershire sauce**

¾ teaspoon freshly ground **black pepper**, plus more to taste

Salt

⅔ cup **canola oil**

3 tablespoons **extra-virgin olive oil**

4 heads **romaine hearts**, leaves separated

EQUIPMENT Food processor or immersion blender and a whisk

In a food processor (or in a tall narrow container if you are using an immersion blender), combine the egg yolks, anchovies (if using), garlic, Parmigiano, lemon juice, mustard, Worcestershire, black pepper, and a pinch of salt. Blend the ingredients until they are combined. With the machine running, slowly drizzle in the canola oil until fully emulsified. Transfer the dressing to a bowl and whisk in the olive oil. Season it to taste with additional salt, pepper, and lemon juice. If the dressing is a bit thinner than you would like for dipping, grate some more cheese into it.

Serve the dressing in a bowl, surrounded by romaine leaves. I recommend keeping extra dressing in the refrigerator and replacing it as needed, rather than leaving the whole batch out. The dressing will keep for about 3 days in the refrigerator, covered.

"Chef Salad" with Cheddar Croutons and Probiotic Ranch

Serves 3 as a main or 4 to 6 as a side

This is my healthy twist on the typical "chef salad" found at many chain restaurants—with the key twist being the Probiotic Ranch (page 79). This is also one of those salads that you should feel emboldened to modify and adapt however you see fit. (My wife, for instance, does not want carrots or bell peppers in her salad, for reasons that she has thus far not properly explained.)

This recipe makes slightly more croutons than you probably need—a convenient scenario when people (including you) begin snacking on them while you make the salad.

....

Cheddar Croutons (recipe follows)

Probiotic Ranch (page 79)

2 heads **lettuce** roughly chopped, such as romaine or red leaf

1 medium **red bell pepper**, cut into bite-size pieces

8 ounces **cucumber**, halved lengthwise and cut crosswise into about ⅛-inch-thick half-moons

1 medium to large **carrot**, grated

5 or 6 very thin slices **red onion**

½ cup **pitted olives**, such as Kalamata or black olives

Salt and freshly ground **black pepper**

EQUIPMENT Grater

Make the croutons and the dressing as directed.

When you are ready to serve the salads, in a large bowl combine the cooled croutons, lettuce, bell pepper, cucumber, carrot, red onion, and olives. Toss them with enough salad dressing to fully coat the leaves. Taste for seasoning, adding more salt and pepper as needed.

Eat the salad immediately.

....

Cheddar Croutons

Makes 4 cups

2½ tablespoons **olive oil**

1 rounded teaspoon **paprika**, (preferably smoked)

1¼ ounces **cheddar cheese**, finely grated

8 ounces **bread**, cut into ¾- to 1-inch cubes

Salt and freshly ground **black pepper**

EQUIPMENT Grater, baking sheet, and parchment paper

Preheat the oven to 425°F. Line a baking sheet with parchment paper.

In a large bowl, combine the olive oil, paprika, and cheddar and swirl it to combine. Add the bread cubes and salt and pepper to taste. Toss them thoroughly to combine. Arrange in a single layer on the lined baking sheet.

Toast the croutons until they are just crisp, but still slightly soft on the interior, about 10 minutes or so, depending on the moisture of the bread.

Season them to taste with more salt and pepper. Allow them to cool to room temperature before using.

Turmeric Tomato Salad with Fried Herbs and Kitchari Spices

Serves 4 to 6

While I generally believe that great summer tomatoes need very little help, this is a fun, flavorful way to add some texture and spice and crunch to them. It also makes excellent use of the cumin seeds, black mustard seeds, and turmeric that you may have already purchased to make Shantam's Kitchari (page 36). The spices get toasted in oil in a pan, and then finished with a handful of green herbs like mint, basil, and cilantro, which crisp up in the golden yellow oil before the whole thing gets poured over sliced tomatoes, where it sizzles and pops to create some very low-key but delicious theater.

This salad is best served right away, in a communal setting, perhaps with some bright, light cocktails or wine.

Any saucepan will work, but the narrower the base the better, as it will allow for a slightly deeper fry.

....

1 pound or so ripe, summer **tomatoes**, cut into about ¼-inch-thick slices

2 tablespoons **cooking oil** (I prefer peanut, but grapeseed, canola, and vegetable will also work)

1 teaspoon **cumin seeds**

1 teaspoon **black mustard seeds**

1 teaspoon ground **turmeric**

½ cup loosely packed assorted soft **herb leaves**, such as mint, basil, cilantro, and parsley

Flaky **sea salt**

Crusty **bread**, for serving

EQUIPMENT Narrow heavy-bottomed saucepan

Lay the sliced tomatoes in a single layer on a serving platter, overlapping them slightly if necessary.

In a narrow heavy-bottomed saucepan, combine the oil, cumin seeds, and black mustard seeds and swirl the pan gently over medium-high heat. Once the spices begin to pop, let them cook for another 30 seconds, paying attention to even the slightest smell of burning—and if there is any, immediately reduce the heat.

Add the turmeric and green herbs and swirl the pan, tilting it slightly and helping to fry the herbs. Fry for about 45 seconds, then immediately pour the oil, herbs, and spices over all of the tomatoes. Season them with flaky sea salt and serve immediately. Serve with crusty bread to sop up any leftover oil and juices.

A Proper Greek Salad

*Serves 1 as a main
or 3 or 4 as a side*

This is less a recipe than it is a public service announcement about Greek salad (horiatiki salata). A traditional, proper Greek salad takes great ingredients and doesn't mess them up. You take a peak-season fresh tomato, some Kalamata olives, cucumber, red onion, and feta cheese and dress with olive oil, salt, pepper, and Greek oregano. That's it.

There is no lettuce. There are no green peppers. There is no vinaigrette.

You should eat this salad with a hunk of crusty bread to soak up all the drips and bits of tomato juice, olive oil, red onion, and feta that have settled together in the bottom of the bowl. This salad is only as good as the ingredients you put into it. If it is December and all you have are pale, hard tomatoes—don't make this salad. Wait until summer.

1 medium **tomato** (10 ounces or so), cut into large bite-size pieces

½ small or ¼ medium **red onion**, cut into fairly thin slices (but not paper thin)

½ cup **Kalamata olives**, pitted or not, depending on preference

1 **English cucumber**, peeled and cut into large bite-size pieces

½ teaspoon **dried Greek oregano**, plus more for sprinkling

3 tablespoons **extra-virgin olive oil**, plus more for drizzling

Salt and freshly ground **black pepper**

3 ounces **feta cheese**

Crusty **bread**, for dipping

In a bowl, combine the tomato, onion, olives, cucumber, oregano, and olive oil. Season with salt and pepper, keeping in mind that the olives and feta are already quite salty. Gently toss all of the ingredients together. Transfer to a serving bowl and top with a slab or dollops of feta cheese. Drizzle the feta with more olive oil and sprinkle on some more oregano. Eat immediately, with bread for dipping.

Pantry Seaweed Salad

Serves 4 as a side

I have, for most of my life, enjoyed seaweed for both its flavor and health benefits. But after reading a wonderful book called *Eat Like a Fish* by Bren Smith, I became fascinated by the holistic benefits of vertical ocean farming—more specifically, the farming of sea vegetables. I highly recommend reading the book rather than getting your information from this headnote, but suffice to say that seaweed farming on a large scale can produce massive quantities of incredibly nutritious food while also improving the ecosystem of our oceans and the planet as a whole.

Also, dried seaweed is completely shelf stable, meaning that you can keep nutritious sea vegetables in your pantry and make a salad with them whenever you want. This version is a bit of a riff on the classic Japanese version found in many grocery stores and restaurants (often just sold as "wakame," a reference to a specific type of seaweed), but while those versions are often quite sweet, I have kept the sugar out of mine entirely. I find that a bit of mustard powder brightens it up and covers for the lack of sugar.

There are many, many different types of sea vegetables out there, each with different textures and colors, and I recommend looking in your local natural foods stores, supermarkets, and online to find different types and see what you like.

NOTE Dried seaweed sheets (often called nori, or snacking seaweed) will not work well for this.

1 ounce dried **wakame,** or "seaweed salad mix"

⅛ teaspoon **mustard powder**

2 tablespoons **tamari**

2 tablespoons **rice vinegar**

1 tablespoon **sesame oil**

1 teaspoon grated or finely minced fresh **ginger**

1 teaspoon toasted **white sesame seeds**, freshly toasted or purchased already roasted

EQUIPMENT Sieve

Completely submerge the dried seaweed in cold water and let soak for 7 minutes.

Meanwhile, in a medium bowl, combine the mustard powder and just a splash of the tamari. Whisk them together to help remove any clumps from the mustard powder, then add the rest of the tamari, the vinegar, sesame oil, ginger, and sesame seeds and whisk just to combine.

Drain the seaweed and squeeze out any excess moisture with your hands. Add the hydrated seaweed to the bowl and mix it together. This can be eaten right away, or stored covered in the refrigerator for 4 days or so. I find that the seaweed salad is best eaten about an hour after being dressed.

pasta and noodles

(and the sauces that go with them, which you can make in large quantities to freeze)

← Drunken Late-Night Pantry Pasta, page 107

Basic Tomato Sauce

(for simple pasta marinara—don't buy jarred sauce)

Serves 2 or 3

This is my quick, easy, everyday tomato sauce. It is chunky, bright, rustic, and designed to be cooked in the time it takes to boil water and cook pasta. It also has a lot of personalized modifiers, based on what you have on hand. My favorite version has fresh basil and chopped parsley—but the truth is, I frequently make this with dried herbs when I haven't been shopping in a while.

For a decadent flourish, I will add a knob of butter at the very end as it is finishing up—this is highly recommended.

While Iliza's Tomato Sauce (page 96) is the one that I will make a large batch of and freeze, this one I only make when I'm going to eat it right away. Doubling this recipe is highly encouraged if you are feeding more people, or are just especially hungry.

....

Salt

1 (28-ounce) can **whole peeled tomatoes**

1½ tablespoons **extra-virgin olive oil**

2 **garlic cloves**, thinly sliced or chopped (I prefer thinly sliced)

Pinch of **crushed red pepper**

¼ teaspoon **dried oregano**

Handful of fresh **basil leaves** or ½ teaspoon dried basil

Freshly ground **black pepper**

2 tablespoons finely chopped fresh **flat-leaf parsley** (optional)

Pasta and Serving

12 ounces dried **pasta**, any kind you like (though my favorite is spaghetti)

1½ tablespoons **unsalted butter** (optional)

Parmigiano-Reggiano, or any hard aged cheese you like

Extra-virgin olive oil, for drizzling

More fresh **basil**, to finish

EQUIPMENT Large pot to boil pasta, a large skillet (large enough to fit both the sauce and cooked pasta), and a colander

Bring a pot of water to a boil over high heat for the pasta. Salt the water generously.

Meanwhile, pour the canned tomatoes and their juices into a bowl and crush them by hand—being careful not to let them pop and explode their juice—until you have a rough, chunky texture with no huge pieces. (If you are squeamish about crushing tomatoes by hand, you can chop them on a cutting board, but try crushing them by hand! It's easy.)

In a large skillet, heat the olive oil over medium heat until it is shimmering. Add the garlic and a pinch of salt and sauté until the garlic is just barely turning brown at the edges. Add the crushed red pepper, oregano, and the basil: If using dried basil, add all of it, if using fresh, add 2 or 3 leaves (the rest will go in at the end). Toast the herbs for about 30 seconds. Add the tomatoes and all of their juices, being careful of splatter. Season the tomatoes with salt and pepper, stir, and add the parsley (if using). Bring to a gentle simmer and continue simmering on low, stirring occasionally, while you cook the pasta.

Cook the pasta: Add the pasta to the boiling water and cook to about 1 minute shy of the package directions. Reserving a little of the pasta cooking water, drain the pasta and add it to the skillet of sauce. Simmer briefly, adding the butter (if using), and a splash of reserved pasta water.

Serve with grated Parmigiano, a drizzle of olive oil, and some roughly torn fresh basil leaves.

Basic Tomato Sauce (top), page 94, and Iliza's Tomato Sauce (bottom), page 96

Iliza's Tomato Sauce

A double batch, serving 3 to 5 people (depending how much pasta you eat) with each batch— or a large batch serving 6 to 10

It took many small tweaks over the years before I found the version of tomato sauce that my wife likes the best. Unlike the chunky, rustic Basic Tomato Sauce (page 94) that I grew up on, this is a little bit more of a restaurant-style sauce, fortified with lots of oil and garlic, steeped with fresh basil, and blended into an almost creamy, emulsified tomato sauce. While the chunky homestyle sauce is what I would cook for myself, this is the sauce that I would serve to other people.

It is very easy, in that you don't have to dirty a bowl or your hands crushing the tomatoes, but takes a little bit of extra time and requires blending (ideally with an immersion blender, directly in the pot). It freezes exceedingly well though, so I recommend making a big batch and keeping deli pints of it in the freezer. Iliza claims that she doesn't have any "comfort foods," but once, when she was not feeling well, she requested this sauce, poured over angel hair pasta, three nights in a row. So . . . you tell me.

This recipe is essentially a double batch, so it calls for freezing half of the sauce for another day—though if you are feeding a crowd, simply cook all of it and double the amount of pasta.

¼ cup **extra-virgin olive oil**

5 **garlic cloves**, smashed with the side of a knife and peeled

1 sprig fresh **basil**

Pinch of **crushed red pepper**

Freshly ground **black pepper**

2 (28-ounce) cans **whole peeled tomatoes**

Salt

Pasta and Serving

Half of the **sauce** (about 3 cups), or more if you prefer a saucy pasta

Salt

1 pound dried **pasta**

Freshly grated **cheese**, such as Parmesan or pecorino

A few leaves of fresh **basil** (optional)

EQUIPMENT Dutch oven or heavy-bottomed pot, immersion blender or stand blender, large pot to boil pasta, and a colander

In a Dutch oven or other heavy-bottomed pot, heat the olive oil and garlic over medium-high heat. Tilt the pan to create a pocket of oil in the corner of the pot that covers the garlic cloves completely—this is basically a way to fully submerge and cook the whole garlic cloves without needing to use an absurd quantity of oil. Move the garlic cloves so that they are completely submerged under the oil—you can even add a tiny bit more oil if necessary.

Maintain the heat so that the garlic cloves release tiny bubbles—you are essentially doing a quick confit without deep-frying them or causing the oil to smoke. Continue until you have some light browning around the edges of the garlic, about 4 minutes.

Return the pan to its normal, upright position. Add the basil sprig and stir it, allowing it to wilt in the oil for about 1 minute. Add the crushed red pepper and a few twists of black pepper and toast them for 30 seconds in the pan. Add the tomatoes and their juices directly from the cans, getting out as much liquid as possible, while being careful not to splash them in the oil. Stir and increase the heat to a strong simmer, then reduce the heat to medium-low, cover the pot, and simmer for 15 minutes, stirring occasionally.

Remove the pan from the heat. Use a pair of tongs, or a fork, to lift the basil from the sauce and discard it (don't worry if a few leaves fell off the stem and are left behind). Blend the sauce with an immersion blender in the pot. (Alternatively, transfer it to a large stand blender and blend it.) Taste for salt and pepper and adjust as you like. Transfer half of the sauce (about 3 cups) to an airtight container (or two deli pints), allow it to come to room temperature, and then store it in the refrigerator or freezer.

Cook the pasta: Bring a large pot of water to a boil. Generously salt the water. Add the pasta and cook until about 1 minute shy of the package directions. Reserving some of the pasta cooking water, drain the pasta and add it to the sauce with a splash of reserved pasta water and simmer briefly together. Serve with grated cheese and a few leaves of fresh basil.

Turkey Pasta

A double batch, serving 3 to 5 people (depending how much pasta you eat) with each batch— or a large batch serving 6 to 10

When I was growing up in California in the '80s and '90s, my mom wanted to serve us a "healthier" version of the meat sauce her mom used to cook for her in Schenectady, New York, substituting ground turkey for beef and pork. My version has evolved over the years, and it has become one of my absolute favorite comfort foods in the world. Dark meat or white will work for this recipe (Iliza prefers white, which miraculously, does not dry out in this recipe).

Unlike a rich, fatty, six-hour winter Bolognese, this is that sauce's bright, light, acidic cousin that cooks in less than 30 minutes. It is supposed to be saucy and a little loose, and you are encouraged to lift up the bowl to your face at the end and slurp up any sauce left at the bottom.

It's also not a very meat-heavy sauce. But since most ground turkey comes in 1-pound packages, this recipe is essentially a double batch, which is great because leftover sauce freezes well. I encourage you to make the full batch, and only cook as much pasta as you are going to eat right away, freezing the rest of the sauce for a weeknight when you don't feel like cooking.

NOTE Any short dried pasta will do, like rigatoni, farfalle, fusilli, and the like—but if you want to really do it right, eat it with wagon wheels like I did as a kid (and still do).

1 medium **carrot**, roughly chopped

1 **celery stalk**, roughly chopped

½ cup loosely packed fresh **flat-leaf parsley**

1 small **onion** or ½ medium onion, roughly chopped

3 **garlic cloves**, peeled

3 tablespoons **olive oil**

1 pound ground **turkey**

½ teaspoon **dried oregano**

⅛ teaspoon **crushed red pepper**, or more to taste

½ cup dry **white wine**

2 (28-ounce) cans **whole peeled tomatoes**

Salt and freshly ground **black pepper**

Pasta and Serving

Salt

12 ounces dried **pasta**

Half of the **Turkey Pasta sauce** →

In a food processor, combine the carrot, celery, parsley, onion, and garlic and blend until you have a well-combined paste with just a bit of rough texture—it will be quite wet from the onion. (Lidia Bastianich calls this a pestata.) If you don't have a food processor, or don't want to use it, you can simply chop all of these ingredients as finely as possible.

In a large skillet or Dutch oven, heat 2 tablespoons of the olive oil over medium-high heat. Add all of the pestata and stir regularly, until most of the liquid has evaporated out, about 5 minutes.

Meanwhile, in a medium bowl, combine the turkey, oregano, crushed red pepper, and white wine and stir to combine (I use my hands and then, obviously, wash them). The turkey will absorb the white wine and become very loose and soft.

Transfer the canned tomatoes to a large bowl, including all of their juices. Crush them by hand until you have a rough, rustic texture, being careful not to squirt tomato juice across the counter and your shirt.

Once the pestata is dry, add the turkey mixture to the pot and stir everything to combine. Add the remaining 1 tablespoon olive oil and season liberally with salt and black pepper. Stir frequently, not worrying at all about browning the turkey, until the turkey is cooked through and the white wine has evaporated, 8 to 10 minutes.

Meanwhile, bring a large pot of water to a boil for the pasta.

Once the turkey is cooked through, add the crushed tomatoes. I like to use a rubber spatula or my hands to scrape all the juice that is stuck to the sides of the bowl. →

← A few leaves fresh **basil** (optional), roughly torn

Freshly ground **black pepper**

Freshly grated **Parmesan** or **pecorino cheese**

Extra-virgin olive oil

EQUIPMENT Food processor (or a willingness to very finely chop by hand), a large skillet or Dutch oven (large enough to fit both the sauce and cooked pasta) with a lid, a large pot for boiling pasta, and a colander

← Stir the sauce to combine and season it lightly with salt and pepper. Bring the sauce to a simmer and then continue simmering, partially covered, for about 10 minutes (about as long as it takes to cook pasta).

Cook the pasta: Bring a large pot of water to a boil. Salt the boiling water and taste it—it should be salted like a well-seasoned broth. Add the pasta and cook it to about 1 minute shy of the package directions. Meanwhile, transfer half of the sauce to an airtight container (or two deli pints), and allow it to come to room temperature before storing it in the refrigerator or freezer.

Drain the pasta and transfer it to the pot of sauce. Increase the heat to medium-high, stirring constantly. Add some fresh basil leaves and continue simmering the pasta until the sauce is fully combined and just barely loose. Taste for seasoning and add more salt and pepper as needed.

To serve, ladle into bowls, top with Parmesan cheese and a drizzle of extra-virgin olive oil.

As with all the brothy pasta dishes (or soups) in this book, just cook the amount of pasta that you want to eat right away. Save the rest of the sauce or broth for leftovers with freshly cooked pasta. Otherwise, the pasta will absorb all the liquid, and you will have overcooked pasta and not enough broth.

Broccoli Pasta

Serves 3 to 5, depending on how much pasta you eat

If there was a holy trinity of pastas in my mom's house growing up, they were Turkey Pasta (page 97), spaghetti with Basic Tomato Sauce (page 94), and Broccoli Pasta (that's this one!). We almost never ate pork or red meat in the house back then, so this vegetarian version of broccoli pasta was a staple of my youth—usually made with orecchiette, but other short-ish pastas like rigatoni, fusilli, and even wagon wheels work really well. The broccoli is meant to be cooked down into a near-pesto consistency, fortified with lots of garlic, made saucy through the use of the all-important starchy pasta water, and finished with cheese, fresh basil, and olive oil.

The most annoying part of making this dish is chopping up all the broccoli florets into fairly small pieces—broccoli is messy—it likes to erupt, leaping from the cutting board and immediately landing all over the counter and floor. My advice is to chop up only a couple of florets at a time so that you can contain their rebellion, and then transfer them to a bowl and start on the next ones.

NOTE Broccoli loves fat. The ¼ cup olive oil will seem like quite a lot until you add the broccoli, and then you will think, "Dear God, I think I need to add more oil." But if you were to keep adding oil, you would find that the broccoli would eventually release all of that oil back into the pan and you would have too much. The trick here is to use a little bit of water when the pan dries out, but not so much as to waterlog the sauce.

Salt

¼ cup **olive oil**

6 **garlic cloves**, chopped

½ teaspoon **dried oregano**

⅛ teaspoon **crushed red pepper**, or to taste

About 6 cups well-chopped **broccoli florets** (from 3 medium or 2 large stalks—save the stems for Veggie Scrap Frittata, page 29, or Veggie Scrap Fried Rice, page 149)

Freshly ground **black pepper**

Pasta and Serving

1 pound dried **pasta**

½ cup or so sliced fresh basil leaves (optional)

Freshly grated **Parmesan** or **pecorino cheese** (or omit to make this vegan)

Extra-virgin olive oil

Bring a large pot of water to a boil for the pasta and add just a moderate amount of salt (you will be using a fair amount of the pasta cooking water in the sauce and you don't want to oversalt the final dish).

In a large skillet or Dutch oven heat the olive oil over medium heat until it is shimmering. Add the garlic and stir. Season the garlic lightly with salt and allow it to brown just a bit around the edges, about 2 minutes. Add the oregano and crushed red pepper and toast them for about 30 seconds.

Tip the broccoli into the skillet, season it with a pinch of salt and some freshly ground black pepper and stir it all together to combine. Once the pan seems dry, scoop about ¼ cup water out of the pasta and into the skillet. Cover with a tight-fitting lid, reduce the heat to medium-low, and cook for 5 minutes to help wilt and steam the broccoli. Uncover and increase the heat to medium-high.

Cook the pasta: Add the pasta to the boiling water and cook to 1 minute shy of the package directions. As the pasta cooks, whenever the skillet of broccoli begins to dry out and brown, add a ladle of pasta water and continue stirring it occasionally. Continue cooking and ladling pasta water as needed, until the broccoli is quite soft, like a pesto. Once it reaches that consistency, reduce the heat to low and stop adding more water.

When the pasta is al dente, drain it and transfer it to the skillet, making sure to reserve at least 1 cup or more of pasta water.

Return the skillet to medium-high heat and stir the pasta and broccoli together, adding more ladles of pasta water as needed until you have a glossy, cohesive pasta dish. If you are using basil leaves, you can toss them in now and give the pasta one more stir. Taste the pasta for seasoning and adjust it as you desire.

Serve immediately, topped with freshly grated cheese (if using) and some olive oil.

Broccoli-Sausage Pasta

Serves 3 to 5, depending on how much pasta you eat

Broccoli and sausage are a classic combination, and one that appears in this book one other time as well, in the form of the Broccoli-Sausage Bread (page 64). The fat of the sausage is cut with white wine and then finds its way into the broccoli before surrounding the pasta and creating one of my favorite flavors in the world.

The use of the homemade sausage, while not required, is highly encouraged.

Salt

Cal-Italian Pork Sausage (page 15) or 1 pound Italian sweet sausage, casings removed

⅓ cup dry **white wine**

2 tablespoons **olive oil**

4 **garlic cloves**, chopped

½ teaspoon **dried oregano**

⅛ teaspoon **crushed red pepper**, or to taste

About 6 cups well-chopped **broccoli florets** (from 3 medium or 2 large stalks—save the stems for Veggie Scrap Frittata, page 29, or Veggie Scrap Fried Rice, page 149)

Freshly ground **black pepper**

Pasta and Serving

Salt

1 pound dried **pasta**

½ cup or so sliced fresh **basil leaves** (optional)

Freshly grated **Parmesan** or **pecorino cheese** (optional, but recommended)

Extra-virgin olive oil

EQUIPMENT Large pot for boiling pasta, large skillet or Dutch oven (large enough to fit both the sauce and cooked pasta), and a colander

Bring a large pot of water to a boil. Generously salt it (it should taste like a well-seasoned broth).

Meanwhile, in a large bowl, combine the sausage and white wine, mixing it together until it is fully combined—the sausage will absorb all of the moisture fairly quickly.

In a large skillet or Dutch oven, heat the olive oil over medium-high heat until it is shimmering. Add the sausage, breaking it up with a wooden spoon as it goes along, and allow it to fry until the raw color is gone and the wine has evaporated, about 4 minutes.

Add the garlic, oregano, and crushed red pepper and stir to combine. Continue sautéing until the liquid is evaporated and the sausage begins to brown around the edges, about 8 minutes.

Add the broccoli and season it with salt and pepper. Stir it well and once it is sizzling, reduce the heat to medium. Continue cooking until the broccoli is quite soft, another 8 minutes or so. If the pan gets too dry, add a splash of water from the pasta pot and deglaze the pan, as needed.

Cook the pasta: Add the pasta to the boiling water and cook it to about 1 minute shy of the package directions. Reserving at least 1 cup of the pasta water, drain the pasta and transfer it to the skillet. Increase the heat to medium-high and stir the pasta and broccoli together, adding ladles of pasta water as needed until you have a glossy, cohesive pasta dish. If you are using basil leaves, you can toss them in now and give the pasta one more stir. Taste the pasta for seasoning and adjust it as you desire.

Serve immediately, topped with freshly grated cheese (if using) and olive oil.

Broccoli-Anchovy Pasta

Serves 3 to 5, depending on how much pasta you eat

Anchovies are divisive. This is based entirely, I think, on people disagreeing with the look of a small fish. But they are highly nutritious, and like many small fish, are high in omega-3 fatty acids, low in mercury, and quite sustainable. They are a perfect pantry staple to keep on hand, when using the canned or jarred types.

Luckily, anchovies are also delicious, adding a salty, umami punch to this pasta that people often cannot quite put their finger on. They fry up and dissolve in the oil, adding sustainable, shelf-stable protein to your dinner. I also sneak in a little soy sauce, just to ramp up those flavors and balance out the lack of cheese (though by all means, finish this with cheese if you are inclined—I would recommend pecorino).

Salt

3 tablespoons **olive oil**

4 **garlic cloves**, chopped

4 oil-packed **anchovy fillets**

½ teaspoon **dried oregano**

⅛ teaspoon **crushed red pepper**, or to taste

1 teaspoon **soy sauce**

About 6 cups well-chopped **broccoli florets** (from 3 medium or 2 large stalks— save the stems for Veggie Scrap Frittata, page 29, or Veggie Scrap Fried Rice, page 149)

Freshly ground **black pepper**

¼ cup dry **white wine**

Pasta and Serving

1 pound dried **pasta**

Salt and freshly ground **black pepper**

Extra-virgin olive oil

EQUIPMENT Pot large enough to boil pasta, large skillet or Dutch oven (large enough to fit both the sauce and cooked pasta), and a colander

Bring a large pot of water to a boil. Salt it generously (it should taste like a well-seasoned broth).

In a large skillet or Dutch oven, heat the olive oil over medium-high heat until it is shimmering. Add the garlic and anchovies and fry them, stirring frequently, for 2 minutes. Add the oregano, crushed red pepper, and soy sauce and allow them to toast for about 30 seconds. Add the broccoli and season it with salt and pepper, stirring the mixture occasionally. Once it is sizzling and the broccoli has absorbed all of the moisture, add the white wine and deglaze the pan, scraping up any browned bits from the bottom of the pan. When the wine has mostly evaporated, reduce the heat to medium and continue stirring occasionally. If the pan becomes too dry, add a splash of boiling pasta water, as needed.

Cook the pasta: Once the broccoli is tender but not completely soft, add the pasta to the boiling water and cook until it is al dente, about 1 minute short of where you want it to end up. Reserving at least 1 cup of the pasta water, drain the pasta and transfer it to the skillet. Increase the heat to medium-high and stir the pasta and broccoli together, adding ladles of pasta water as needed until you have a glossy, cohesive pasta dish. Taste the pasta for seasoning and add salt as needed.

Serve immediately, topped with lots of freshly ground black pepper and olive oil.

Pasta with Rosemary-Bacon Tomato Sauce

Serves 3 to 5, depending on how much pasta you eat

This dish came about because we had an episode of the show coming up and I looked around in the fridge and said, "Okay, I have 2 slices of bacon, a little bit of white wine, and some rosemary." The result was a hit among the fans of the show—a pasta that's simultaneously earthy, bright, herbaceous, savory, and frankly, just really, really good.

I love using just a little bit of bacon to flavor a whole dish, rather than making it a "meat sauce." As always, I preach for "less and better" when it comes to meat, so buying a high-quality bacon and using it sparingly is highly recommended. There are also "keto" bacons on the market now that don't have any added sugar.

Salt

2 slices **bacon**, cut into ¼-inch slices

2 teaspoons **olive oil**

1 medium **onion**, diced (I prefer red onion in this dish)

2 **garlic cloves**, chopped

Freshly ground **black pepper**

Pinch of **crushed red pepper**

3 sprigs fresh **rosemary**

½ cup dry **white wine**

1 (28-ounce) can **whole peeled tomatoes**, crushed by hand

Pasta and Serving

1 pound dried **pasta** (I really like this with fusilli or rigatoni, but any will do)

Freshly grated **Parmesan, pecorino**, or a similar sharp, aged cheese

Extra-virgin olive oil

EQUIPMENT Pot large enough to boil pasta, a large skillet or Dutch oven, and a colander

Bring a pot of water to a boil and season it like a well-salted broth.

Set a large skillet or Dutch oven over medium heat. Add the bacon and allow to begin rendering, stirring occasionally, until roughly halfway cooked, 6 to 9 minutes.

Increase the heat to medium-high and add the oil, onion, and garlic and stir. Season with salt and black pepper. Continue sautéing until the onion, garlic, and bacon are browned around the edges, about 5 minutes longer.

Add the crushed red pepper and rosemary sprigs and stir. Toast for 30 seconds and then add the white wine and scrape the bottom of the pan to deglaze any browned bits. Allow to simmer until the liquid is mostly evaporated.

Add the tomatoes, season with salt and pepper, and stir. Once it is bubbling, reduce the heat to a simmer and continue simmering, covered, for about 10 minutes.

Cook the pasta: Meanwhile, add the pasta to the boiling water and cook to about 1 minute shy of the package directions.

Reserving a cup or so of pasta water, drain the pasta and transfer it to the pan with the sauce. Increase the heat to a steady simmer and stir constantly, adding a splash of pasta water as needed to get a sauce that fully coats the pasta without being soupy or overly dry, 1 to 2 minutes. Taste for seasoning and adjust.

Serve immediately in bowls, topped with cheese and a drizzle of olive oil.

Pasta with Rosemary-Mushroom Tomato Sauce

Serves 3 to 5, depending on how much pasta you eat

I wanted to make a vegetarian complement to the Pasta with Rosemary-Bacon Tomato Sauce (page 104), and dried mushrooms seemed like a natural fit. This is a delicious pasta all on its own, using the white wine and tomatoes to add brightness and acidity to balance out the earthy tones of dried mushrooms and rosemary.

NOTE Any dried mushroom will do, but I prefer porcini or shiitake. And for the pasta, any shape will do, but I really like this with fusilli or rigatoni.

....

½ ounce dried **mushrooms**

Salt

1 tablespoon plus 1 teaspoon **olive oil**

1 medium **onion**, diced (I prefer red onion in this dish)

2 **garlic cloves**, chopped

Pinch of **crushed red pepper**

3 sprigs fresh **rosemary**

½ cup dry **white wine**

1 (28-ounce) can **whole peeled tomatoes**, crushed by hand

Freshly ground **black pepper**

Pasta and Serving

1 pound dried **pasta**

Freshly grated **Parmesan**, **pecorino**, or a similar sharp, aged cheese

Extra-virgin olive oil

EQUIPMENT Pot large enough to boil pasta, a skillet or Dutch oven (large enough to fit both the sauce and cooked pasta), and a colander

Place the dried mushrooms in a small bowl and add ½ cup warm water. Allow the mushrooms to soak until fully softened, about 30 minutes. Reserving the soaking water, scoop out the mushrooms, transfer them to a cutting board, and finely chop them.

Bring a large pot of water to a boil for the pasta. Generously salt the water.

In a large skillet or Dutch oven, heat the oil over medium heat. Add the onion, garlic, and a pinch of salt. Sauté, stirring occasionally until the alliums are just wilted, about 2 minutes. Increase the heat to medium-high, add the chopped mushrooms, and sauté, stirring occasionally, until the onions are browning a bit at the edges, 5 to 7 minutes.

Add the crushed red pepper and rosemary sprigs, stir, and toast for 30 seconds. Add the white wine and reserved mushroom soaking liquid (leaving behind any sediment at the bottom of the bowl) and scrape the bottom of the pan with a wooden spoon to deglaze any browned bits. Allow to simmer until the liquid is mostly evaporated.

Add the tomatoes, season with salt and pepper, and stir. Once it is bubbling, reduce the heat to a simmer and continue simmering, covered, for about 10 minutes.

Cook the pasta: Meanwhile, add the pasta to the boiling water and cook to about 1 minute shy of the package directions.

Reserving 1 cup or so of pasta water, drain the pasta and transfer it to the pan with the sauce. Increase the heat to a steady simmer and stir constantly, adding a splash of pasta water as needed to get a sauce that fully coats the pasta without being soupy or overly dry, 1 to 2 minutes. Taste for seasoning and adjust.

Serve immediately in bowls, topped with cheese and a drizzle of olive oil.

Pasta with Shoyu Butter Clam Sauce

Serves 2 or 3

While I have very strong opinions about using tiny fresh clams for pasta vongole, I really wanted to find a version that uses the much more readily available (and consistent) canned ones, which make an excellent pantry staple. The easiest and quickest one turned out to be the clear winner: chopped canned clams sautéed with onions, garlic, butter, olive oil, black pepper, and shoyu (Japanese soy sauce), then spiked with fresh parsley, lemon zest, and lemon juice. The key is to undercook the pasta just a bit and then finish it in the pan with the reserved clam juice, getting all of that delightful briny flavor directly into the noodle itself. Think of this as a cross between spaghetti with clams and the Drunken Late-Night Pantry Pasta (page 107). Spaghetti works very well with this, but I found that my absolute favorite is actually farfalle (bow-tie).

NOTE I prefer to use canned clams that do not have sugar added. But most important: Read the ingredients and make sure that they are packed in clam juice, rather than water. If you cannot find chopped clams, whole clams are fine, too—you will just need to chop them. Also, look at the place of origin (see Seafood Sustainability, page 129).

Salt

1 tablespoon **olive oil**

1 tablespoon **unsalted butter**

½ cup minced **onion**

3 **garlic cloves**, sliced

1½ tablespoons **soy sauce**

2 (6.5-ounce) cans chopped **clams** in clam juice (see Note)

1 teaspoon grated **lemon zest**

Freshly ground **black pepper**

Pasta and Serving

12 ounces dried **pasta**, such as farfalle or spaghetti

2 tablespoons chopped fresh **parsley**

Freshly ground **black pepper**

Extra-virgin olive oil

A squeeze of **lemon juice**

EQUIPMENT Pot large enough to boil pasta, sieve, and a large skillet or Dutch oven (large enough to hold both the sauce and pasta)

Bring a large pot of water to a boil for the pasta. Season it lightly with salt (the soy sauce and clams have a fair amount of salt already, so you will want to be cautious).

In a large skillet or Dutch oven, heat the oil and butter over medium heat until the butter is melted. Add the onion, garlic, and soy sauce and fry gently until the onion is fully wilted, about 3 minutes.

Set a sieve over a bowl—the bowl will be there to catch the clam juice. Open the cans of clams and pour them into the sieve, reserving the juice. (If the clams are whole, chop them up into small pieces.)

Add the lemon zest to the skillet and stir gently. Add the chopped clams and season liberally with black pepper. Reduce the heat to low and stir them occasionally.

Cook the pasta: Meanwhile, add the pasta to the boiling water and stir. Set a timer for about 2 minutes short of the recommended cooking time.

Once the timer goes off, add the clam juice to the skillet with the clams and increase the heat to high. Reserving some of the pasta water (in case you need it), immediately drain the pasta and transfer it to the pan. Simmer it together with the clam mixture, stirring constantly, until the clam juice is absorbed into the pasta. If the juice is absorbed and the pasta is not cooked to your desired texture, add a little reserved pasta water and keep cooking for a minute or two longer. Stir in the parsley and more black pepper and toss it together.

To serve, transfer it to bowls and eat it immediately, topped with a drizzle of olive oil and a squeeze of lemon.

Drunken Late-Night Pantry Pasta

Serves 1

Somewhere along the line, this became the pasta that I would cook for myself if I got home late from a night of drinking with friends and did not manage to get tacos first. This is a recipe for one, since my night out drinking with friends usually only happens when my wife is on the road.

(When my wife is out of town, I mostly have two options: meet a friend for a drink and stay out until last call; or stay home, cook dinner, watch a movie, and go to bed at 9:30.)

But I digress. This is about the delightful combination of soy sauce and butter, which, when added to pasta with some of the reserved pasta water, become a starchy pot of salty, fatty perfection, usually spiced up with a bit of shichimi. It is often eaten while standing in the kitchen, directly out of the pot.

6 ounces dried **pasta** (I love this with rigatoni, but any will do)

Salt

1½ tablespoons **unsalted butter**

1½ tablespoons **soy sauce**

Dried spices of your choosing, such as freshly ground black pepper, a few shakes of shichimi, ground sanshō pepper, or nothing at all

Parmigiano-Reggiano, or a sharp aged cheese of your choice (optional), for serving

A light squeeze of **lemon juice** (optional, but nice)

EQUIPMENT Medium pot or saucepan, a sieve, and a mug

Fill the pot with just enough water to cover the pasta by an inch or so. Bring to a boil with a pinch of salt (if you are sensitive to salt, you can leave the salt out and adjust later as needed, due to the soy sauce in this recipe).

Add the pasta and stir occasionally until the pasta is al dente, or about 30 seconds short of your desired doneness. Reserving a mug of the starchy pasta water, drain the pasta and return it to the pot.

Add about ½ cup of the pasta water to the pot and return it to medium-high heat. Add the butter, soy sauce, and your choice of spices, stirring constantly until the butter has emulsified with the soy sauce and thickened up. You should end up with a glossy pot of coated pasta.

Top with cheese or a squeeze of lemon if you desire. Taste it for seasoning and adjust as needed, then eat it immediately, being careful not to burn your mouth.

Pasta Fazool

Serves about 3

Some people got through college by eating instant ramen or boxed macaroni and cheese. I made Pasta Fazool. I have probably cooked this dish, in one iteration or another, more than anything I've ever made in my life. This is not the more well-known version of Pasta e Fagioli that includes things like chicken stock, pancetta, and diced vegetables. This is my family's "Pasta Fazool," an Italian-American way of saying pasta and beans, and a complete meal that lies somewhere between soup and tomato sauce, which can be thrown together in less than 30 minutes, using mostly things that come in a can, bottle, or box, making it a pantry winner; and the reason that there are always dried pasta, canned tomatoes, and canned white beans in my kitchen.

I tend to put some form of a green vegetable in mine, but if you don't have it you can just skip it and you will make a very good bowl of fazool. Fresh basil is great as well, but can also be skipped. If I haven't been shopping in a long time, or have just flown in from out of town, I have happily made this with an old bulb of garlic being the closest thing to a fresh ingredient.

NOTE As with all the brothy pasta dishes (or soups) in this book, just cook the amount of pasta that you want to eat right away. Save the rest of the sauce/broth for leftovers with freshly cooked pasta, as otherwise you'll have mushy leftovers.

NOTE 2 This recipe doubles well for a larger group.

....

2 (28-ounce) cans **whole peeled tomatoes**

2 tablespoons **olive oil**

3 **garlic cloves**, sliced

1 head of **escarole** or **spinach**, washed and roughly chopped, or 1 (8-ounce) bag of baby spinach (you can omit the greens, in a pinch)

Salt and freshly ground **black pepper**

1¾ cups homemade cooked **beans** with their cooking liquid (page 2), or 1 (15-ounce) can beans (cannellini or any white bean works great), undrained

1 teaspoon **dried oregano**

12 ounces (or as much as you are going to eat in one sitting) medium dried **soup pasta**—orecchiette or medium shells are my favorite →

Bring a large pot of water to a boil for the pasta.

Meanwhile, pour the canned tomatoes and their juices into a large bowl. I often use a rubber spatula to get all of the juices out of the can. Crush the tomatoes with your (clean!) hands, being careful every time you burst a whole tomato as the juice really wants to squirt all across your kitchen and your shirt. Remove any especially hard stem chunks or bits of skin and discard. Your tomatoes should end up with a coarse, chunky consistency.

In the Dutch oven, heat the olive oil over medium heat until shimmering. Add the garlic and sauté until it is just starting to brown around the edges, 1 to 2 minutes. Increase the heat to medium-high. If using greens, add them now (or skip straight to adding the beans), season lightly with salt and pepper and cook until fully wilted. Add the beans (with their juices), oregano, and a little salt and pepper and let them simmer, stirring frequently, until the liquid has thickened nicely and reduced by about half.

Add the crushed tomatoes, scraping out as much of the juices from the sides of the bowl as you can. Stir the tomatoes and then season them with more salt and pepper. Continue cooking over medium-high heat until everything is simmering, then cover and reduce the heat to a gentle simmer while you cook the pasta.

By now, the water should be boiling. Season it with salt until it tastes like a nicely flavored broth, then add the pasta and cook until just al dente according to the package directions. →

← 1½ cups loosely packed fresh **basil leaves** (optional), roughly torn

Freshly grated **Parmesan cheese**, for serving

Extra-virgin olive oil, for serving

EQUIPMENT Pot large enough to boil pasta and a Dutch oven or heavy-bottomed soup pot with a lid

← If serving all the fazool at once Drain the pasta and then add it to the pot with the tomatoes and beans. Toss in half of the fresh basil and stir, allowing everything to simmer together briefly and combine. Taste for seasoning and adjust as desired. Ladle into three soup bowls and top with Parmesan cheese, olive oil, and fresh basil. Eat immediately, with a soup spoon.

If only eating some of the fazool Drain the pasta and return it to the pot that you cooked it in. Return it to the stove over medium heat and ladle in enough of the tomato-bean broth to make a balanced soup. Toss in some of the fresh basil and stir, allowing everything to simmer together briefly and combine. Taste for seasoning and adjust as desired, then ladle into soup bowls and top with Parmesan cheese, olive oil, and fresh basil. Eat immediately, with a soup spoon.

Allow leftover fazool to cool and then cover and store in the refrigerator for up to 1 week.

Warm Heirloom Summer Fazool

Serves 5 to 7, depending on how much pasta you eat

Heirloom tomatoes are seductive. They curve and protrude, presenting their bright colors on farmers market tables. When I first saw one I thought, "Oh, this is what tomatoes were always supposed to be." But then I tried to make some into a tomato sauce and I realized that heat only made them watery and overly sweet. I've since decided that in most cases, heirloom tomatoes are best eaten raw, on a piece of bread, or in things like A Proper Greek Salad (page 89).

This, however, is the exception. Here is my summer pasta fazool: small pasta and white beans sit in an heirloom tomato broth that veers somewhere between gazpacho and tomato sauce, eaten warm, and able to be enjoyed on a hot summer day. But it really has one goal—to suspend the flavor of raw, peak-of-the-season heirloom tomatoes, while infusing them with the flavor of slow-cooked garlic and basil.

Admittedly, confiting (slow cooking in oil) garlic cloves and basil sprigs, and then blanching and peeling tomatoes, seems like a lot of work to eat a tomato. But I've come to realize that this is also my absolute favorite way to preserve the flavor of heirloom tomatoes.

NOTE This recipe also freezes exceedingly well, allowing you to taste the peak of summer several months after it has ended. Should you find yourself with an excess of heirloom tomatoes, this recipe can be doubled or tripled or even quadrupled. Once you have the sauce on hand, you can cook the pasta and reheat beans and you have summer fazool on the fly. Just try to thaw the broth in the refrigerator a day or two before you want to eat it, as using a microwave or stovetop for thawing will zap the flavor.

Like with regular Pasta Fazool (page 109), make as much sauce as you want, but only cook as much pasta and beans as you're going to eat in one sitting (the ideal ratio is 2 cups of sauce to a ½ pound of pasta and a 15-ounce can of beans).

6 **garlic cloves**, thinly sliced

½ cup **extra-virgin olive oil**

2 sprigs **basil**, leaves picked from stems, stems and leaves kept separate

4 pounds (or slightly more) ripe **heirloom tomatoes**

Salt (this is actually a good place to use fancy salt if you really want to)

1 pound small dried **pasta shapes**, such as tubetti, ditalini, or small shells

3½ cups cooked **white beans** or 2 (15-ounce) cans white beans, drained

Freshly ground **black pepper** →

Start by making the infused oil. In a small saucepan, combine the garlic and oil. The garlic slices should be thin enough that they are totally submerged in oil. If they're not submerged, move them around until coated, or add a little more oil. Add the basil stems (it's okay if they stick out), bending them in half to fit in the pan if necessary. Bring the oil to a gentle bubble (over either low or medium-low heat, depending on your stove), a couple of minutes—if the garlic is sputtering, turn the heat down. Once the basil stems start to wilt, you can push them down into the oil with a fork or a cooking spoon. Continue cooking gently over low heat until the garlic is so tender that you could spread it with a butter knife, about 25 minutes.

Discard the basil stems. Set a sieve over a small bowl and pour the garlic and oil into it. (Save the garlic slices, too: They are delicious sprinkled on top of the pasta at the end, or just spread onto a piece of toast, or in a sandwich.) Set the oil aside. This step can be done several hours or even days in advance.

Next, bring a large pot of water to a boil. It should be big enough to blanch all of your tomatoes without crowding (or blanch them in batches if you don't have a big enough pot). →

← Freshly grated **Parmigiano-Reggiano** cheese (optional)

EQUIPMENT Small saucepan (or any decent pan, as long as it's not very wide), sieve, large pot for blanching tomatoes and boiling pasta, and a blender or immersion blender

← Meanwhile, use a knife to cut a little "X" on the bottom of each tomato (this will make it easier for the skin to release). Once the water is boiling, gently lower each tomato into the boiling water. Blanch for 30 to 60 seconds, or until the skins just begin to soften and pull back around the little "X" you cut. Gently lift the tomatoes out of the water and set aside on a plate or in a bowl. You can reuse this water and this pot to cook the pasta and reheat the beans.

Once cool enough to handle, take each tomato and hold it over a large bowl, allowing any juices to drip into the bowl while handling. Using your fingers, or the back of a knife, peel back the skin and discard it (I will sometimes squeeze any last bits of flesh or juice off the skin first). With a small knife, cut out the hard core of the tomatoes and discard. You'll notice that the center of the tomato is still cold and quite raw. Drop the finished tomato into the bowl and then repeat with the remaining ones.

Season the tomatoes with a hefty pinch of salt. Using an immersion blender right in the bowl (or in a stand blender in batches if necessary) blend the tomatoes until almost completely smooth. It might take a moment to get them started with the immersion blender, but they should quickly begin releasing a lot of liquid.

Once blended, taste for seasoning and adjust. Continue blending and slowly drizzle in the infused oil. Keep blending until all of the oil is poured in. Taste the tomato broth for seasoning and adjust if needed. You will need 5 total cups of tomato broth for the recipe; refrigerate or freeze the remainder.

When it's time to eat, bring the water back up to a boil (or start a new pot of water to boil). Season with salt (it should taste like a nicely seasoned broth). Add the pasta to the water and cook to about 3 minutes shy of the package directions. Add the drained beans to the water and stir. Continue cooking until the pasta is just al dente and then drain completely.

Transfer the hot pasta and beans to a large bowl. Roughly tear the reserved basil leaves and stir them into the hot pasta, allowing them to wilt. Stir the tomato broth, then add 4 cups of the tomato broth to the pasta and stir together.

Ladle into bowls. Top each bowl with the remaining tomato broth. Finish with black pepper and cheese (and confited garlic slices if you held onto them). Eat immediately.

Green Vegetable Pesto

Makes about 3½ cups

As much as I adore a classic pesto Genovese, made from pine nuts, basil, Parmesan, and olive oil—this vegetable-loaded version is one of my favorite ways to use up any extra green vegetables that I have lying around. In fact, I often find myself making a big batch and then freezing it in little containers, almost as a means of pausing fresh spring vegetables and then getting to eat them again a few months later.

Many vegetables will work here—broccoli, snap peas, green peas, fava beans, kale, and the like—anything that will bring a vegetal flavor and bright green color. Even frozen peas work well in a pinch.

This pesto is delicious tossed with freshly cooked pasta (see Green Pesto Pasta, opposite), a little of the pasta water, and some more olive oil and grated cheese. It also is a great accompaniment to a piece of fish, or in the Vegan Minestrone with Miso Pesto (page 126)—which makes it, well, just a Minestrone with Pesto.

Salt

8 ounces **green vegetables**, such as broccoli florets, green peas (shelled fresh or frozen), fava beans, roughly chopped kale, whole snap peas, and the like (2½ to 3 cups)

¼ cup raw **almonds** (1¼ ounces), toasted until fragrant

3 **garlic cloves**, peeled

1 ounce **Parmesan** or any sharp aged cheese you like, freshly grated (about ½ cup)

3 tablespoons fresh **lemon juice**, plus more to taste

¼ cup roughly torn fresh **basil leaves**

3 tablespoons **extra-virgin olive oil**

Freshly ground **black pepper**

EQUIPMENT Large pot to blanch vegetables, sieve, and a food processor or blender (with a tamper)

Bring a large pot of water to a boil and salt well.

Meanwhile, fill a large bowl with ice water—this will be to shock the vegetables after they are cooked, preserving their bright green color and stopping the cooking process.

Drop the vegetables into the boiling water and blanch them until they are just barely cooked but still crisp, about 90 seconds. Immediately drain and then plunge them into the ice bath to cool, stirring them a bit to distribute them in the water. Once they are fully chilled, drain again, discarding the ice. Let them sit in the sieve for a couple of minutes to drain off any excess water (you don't want it to dilute the pesto).

Meanwhile, in a food processor or blender, combine the almonds and garlic and process to a coarse texture similar to bread crumbs. Add the blanched vegetables, grated cheese, lemon juice, basil, olive oil, and a few twists of black pepper. Pulse, scraping down the sides of the bowl as needed, until you have a coarsely textured pesto that is not quite completely smooth. Season to taste with salt and more lemon juice as needed, then transfer it to containers.

Green Pesto Pasta

Serves 3 to 5, depending on how much pasta you eat

Salt

1 pound dried **pasta**

Rounded ½ cup **Green Vegetable Pesto** (page 114)

2 tablespoons **extra-virgin olive oil**

½ cup freshly **grated cheese**, such as Parmigiano-Reggiano

Freshly ground **black pepper**

Bring a large pot of water to a boil and salt well. Add the pasta and cook to al dente according to the package directions. Reserving about ½ cup of the pasta cooking water, drain the pasta and transfer to a large bowl. Toss the cooked pasta, pesto, 3 tablespoons of the reserved pasta water, the olive oil, and cheese. Season it to taste with salt and pepper and then eat it immediately.

Miso-Spinach Pesto

Makes about 2 cups

This recipe came about because my wonderful editor, Lexy Bloom, said to me: "Selfishly, I would like you to add a miso pesto to the book, because most vegan pesto is terrible, but I had one with miso once that was very good." I'm sure this version is quite different from the one she had, but I think it is quite good: It is bright, herbaceous, and beautifully green, bringing a pop of flavor to pasta, soba, fish, and even Vegan Minestrone with Miso Pesto (page 126).

You can pair this pesto with pasta or with soba, an idea that actually came from Sarah Gim (IG: @TheDelicious), who makes her own version of miso pesto with kale. Our friendship, I believe, exists entirely through Instagram direct messages about each other's food photos, and our mutual appreciation for my dog's beauty.

This is best eaten within a few days, but also freezes well if you make too much.

½ cup raw **almonds** (2½ ounces), toasted until fragrant, or store-bought

3 **garlic cloves**, peeled

8 ounces **spinach leaves**

3 tablespoons fresh **lemon juice**

3 tablespoons **white miso**

½ cup loosely packed fresh **basil leaves**

1½ teaspoons **rice vinegar**

1 teaspoon **tamari**

A few twists of **black pepper**

¼ teaspoon **crushed red pepper**

¼ cup **extra-virgin olive oil**

Salt

EQUIPMENT Food processor

In a food processor, pulse the almonds and garlic until you have a very coarsely ground mixture, scraping down the sides of the food processor as needed.

Add the spinach, lemon juice, miso, basil, vinegar, tamari, black pepper, and crushed red pepper and blend until you have a mostly broken down and blended mixture. With the machine running, drizzle in the olive oil and process until the pesto is unified and mostly smooth, with some little bits of texture left behind.

Season to taste with salt and use immediately or store in a tightly sealed container in the refrigerator. →

Miso Pesto Pasta

Serves 3 to 5, depending on how much pasta you eat

Salt

1 pound dried **pasta**

A rounded ½ cup **Miso-Spinach Pesto** (page 117)

2 tablespoons **extra-virgin olive oil**

Freshly ground **black pepper**

Bring a large pot of water to a boil and salt well. Add the pasta and cook to al dente according to the package directions. Reserving about ½ cup of the pasta cooking water, drain the pasta and transfer to a large bowl. Add the pesto and olive oil and toss to combine. Season to taste with salt and black pepper and eat immediately.

Miso Pesto Soba

Serves 1

90 grams (3.2 ounces) dried **soba noodles**

2 tablespoons **Miso-Spinach Pesto** (page 117)

1 teaspoon **extra-virgin olive oil**

Salt

Freshly ground **black pepper**

In a pot of boiling water, cook the soba according to the package directions. Reserving a splash of cooking water, drain the soba and transfer to a serving bowl. Add the pesto, 2 teaspoons reserved cooking water, and the olive oil and toss to combine. Season to taste with salt and pepper and eat immediately.

Cold Sesame Soba

Serves 2 as a main or 3 to 6 as a side

I have very fond memories of eating cold sesame noodles as a kid, from many of the various L.A. Chinese take-out spots—those room-temperature, nutty, salty noodles, clumping together and making squishing sounds when I gathered them with a pair of chopsticks and lifted them from the box.

When I stumbled upon the Vegan Tahini Dressing (page 75) for this book, I frequently found myself tossing it with some soba noodles, which add a nice earthy flavor. While I will admit to enjoying it with just the dressing and soba noodles, this final version is my absolute favorite. The tahini dressing here is tweaked slightly from the original, with a bit of chile oil sneaking its way in.

¼ cup **tahini**

3 tablespoons **extra-virgin olive oil**

1 tablespoon **Chile Oil** (page 17) or sesame oil

1 tablespoon plus 1 teaspoon **tamari**

1 tablespoon plus 1 teaspoon **red wine vinegar**

1 tablespoon plus 1 teaspoon **rice vinegar**

360 grams (12.7 ounces) **soba noodles**

Salt

1 **English cucumber** (about 11 ounces) or 4 Persian (mini) cucumbers, cut into matchsticks about 2½ inches long

2 **scallions**, dark green tops only, sliced

1 tablespoon **white sesame seeds**, freshly roasted or purchased already toasted

EQUIPMENT Large pot for the noodles and a sieve

Bring a large pot of water to a boil for the soba.

Meanwhile, in a large mixing or serving bowl, combine the tahini, olive oil, chile oil, tamari, red wine vinegar, and rice vinegar and stir until combined. (It will look broken at first, but will hydrate and become smooth while it sits.)

Once the water is boiling, cook the soba noodles according to the package directions. Drain the soba in a sieve and rinse them under cold water. Shake the sieve several times, trying to get as much water off the noodles as possible so as not to dilute the dressing.

Add the drained noodles to the bowl of dressing and toss them until they are very well combined. Season to taste with salt, as needed. Then, either in that same bowl or divided into smaller bowls, garnish the soba noodles with julienned cucumbers, scallion greens, and sesame seeds. Eat immediately.

Leftovers will keep in the refrigerator for about 5 days.

Rice Noodle Salad with Kale and Edamame

Serves 1 or 2 as a main or 4 to 6 as a side

This is a fairly quick, simple noodle salad in which the rice noodles and vegetables get boiled together in the same pot, then drained and tossed in dressing. The shredded kale gets pulled up and tangled with the noodles, while the little bits of peas or edamame scramble around, to be picked up and popped into your mouth at your leisure.

This gluten-free and sugar-free noodle salad tastes great right after it is made, or can be kept in the refrigerator and eaten cold later. I find that the tamari and lime juice get a bit muted as they chill down, so if you make this in advance, I recommend doing some final tasting and seasoning right before it is served.

1 tablespoon **sesame oil**

2 tablespoons **tamari**, plus more to taste

1 tablespoon **rice vinegar**

1 **garlic clove**, grated

½ teaspoon grated fresh **ginger**

12 **kale leaves**, midribs and stems discarded

8 ounces **rice noodles**

¼ cup frozen shelled **edamame** or **peas**

Lime juice, to finish

1 tablespoon **white sesame seeds**, freshly roasted or purchased already toasted

¼ cup sliced fresh **cilantro leaves** (optional)

EQUIPMENT Grater (for the ginger and garlic), large pot for the noodles, and a colander

Bring a large pot of water to a boil—you want to give rice noodles plenty of water or else they will get gummy.

In a large bowl, whisk together the sesame oil, tamari, rice vinegar, garlic, and ginger. Slice the kale leaves into strips ½ inch or so wide.

Add the rice noodles and edamame to the boiling water, stirring frequently to prevent the noodles from sticking together. Once the noodles are chewy, tender, and cooked to your liking, stir in the kale shreds. Let the kale cook for about 10 seconds and then drain everything into a colander. Rinse the noodles and vegetables under cold water until they are just warm, then let as much of the water as possible drain off.

Add the noodles and vegetables to the bowl and toss them thoroughly to combine. Season the salad with additional tamari and lime juice to taste. (If you want to serve it later, do not add the tamari and lime juice. Cover and store in the refrigerator, and when you are ready to serve, season it to taste with tamari and lime.)

Serve it in a large bowl or individual bowls, garnished with the toasted sesame seeds and sliced cilantro.

soups and stews

(brothy things, to eat in bowls)

← Vegan Minestrone with Miso Pesto, page 126

Mom's Minestrone

Serves 6 to 8

This is less a soup than it is an Italian-American vegetable stew, great on its own but most often (in my home anyway) eaten so that it is closer to a vegetable stroganoff or Bolognese, coating orecchiette or medium pasta shells with its thick, rustic, vegetable-and-bean gravy, and finished in the bowl with fresh basil and a dusting of Parmesan and olive oil.

It takes longer to cook than you would think it has any right to, and when friends have asked for the recipe, I always give it with this caveat: "As soon as you think it's done, let it cook for another hour." It is somewhere during that time, in which it feels as if the soup has taken a deep breath and dropped its shoulders, and all of the ingredients have sunken into each other, that it is finally a pot of minestrone soup.

It is a fairly malleable soup, and you are welcome to substitute any ingredients for others that you like (cauliflower for potato, kale for zucchini, vegetable stock for chicken stock, red lentils for pasta, etc.), but I refuse to find out what happens if I don't use leeks (which add deep nuance), yellow squash (which dissolve and thicken the broth), or peas (which pop delightfully in your mouth).

Finally, for any soup that has pasta in it, the pasta should be cooked to order for the number of servings you are planning, as otherwise the pasta would get overcooked and soft if left in the pot of soup.

2 tablespoons **olive oil**

2 tablespoons **unsalted butter**

2 **leeks**, white and light-green parts only, washed and diced

2 **garlic cloves**, roughly chopped

Salt and freshly ground **black pepper**

About 1 pound **potatoes**, medium-diced

3 medium or 2 large **carrots**, cut into ¼-inch slices

4 **celery stalks**, cut into ¼-inch slices

2 medium **yellow squash**, halved lengthwise and cut crosswise into ¼-inch half-moons

1 **zucchini**, halved lengthwise and cut crosswise into ¼-inch half-moons

8 ounces **green beans**, ends trimmed, cut into ½-inch pieces

1 pound **frozen peas** (or fresh if you happen to have them)

In a heavy-bottomed soup pot, heat the olive oil and butter over medium-low heat (the goal is to build flavor slowly at first). When the butter has melted, add the leeks and garlic and allow them to sweat slowly. Season them with salt and pepper; stir occasionally (and get used to this step, since you are going to be doing it every time you add a new ingredient) until they have wilted and softened, about 4 minutes.

Remark over how wonderful the kitchen smells, then add the potatoes, season with salt and pepper, stir to combine, and cook until they have just begun to sizzle in the pan. Add the carrots, season, and stir. By now the pan will start to crowd, so you can increase the heat to medium.

Repeat these steps, adding each new ingredient, seasoning, stirring, and allowing to sizzle before moving on to the next, adding in this order: celery, yellow squash, zucchini, green beans, and peas. It should almost look like you are making a vegetable pot pie filling.

Add the beans, including their liquid, season, and stir. Pour in 2 cups water and the chicken stock. Increase the heat to medium-high and add the Parmesan rind, stirring occasionally until the mixture is at a simmer. Finally, add the tomatoes and their juices, seasoning (yes, again) with salt and pepper, and bring the whole pot to a gentle simmer.

Reduce it to a bare simmer and cover the pot. Continue simmering the minestrone, stirring it occasionally, until it has thickened into a hearty stew, about 3 hours. Taste for seasoning and adjust as you see fit.

3½ cups cooked **beans** with their cooking liquid, homemade (page 2), or 2 (15-ounce) cans beans (if I'm using canned beans I usually use a can each of cannellini and red kidney), undrained

2 cups **Chicken Stock** (page 5)

A **Parmesan rind**

1 (28-ounce) can **whole peeled tomatoes**, crushed by hand

Pasta and Serving

Salt

3 to 4 ounces dried **pasta** per person, such as orecchiette or medium shells

Freshly grated **Parmigiano-Reggiano** or a hard aged cheese of your choice

Extra-virgin olive oil

Roughly torn fresh **basil**

EQUIPMENT A heavy-bottomed soup pot (at least 7 quarts) with a lid and a pot for cooking the pasta

Cook the pasta: Bring a pot of water to a boil. Nicely salt the water. Add as much pasta as the number of servings of minestrone you are planning on eating and cook until al dente according to the package directions. Drain the pasta and return it to the pot. Ladle in enough of the minestrone so that it is more of a soup with pasta and allow the mixture to simmer together for about 30 seconds.

To serve, ladle the minestrone into bowls and top each one with cheese, olive oil, and basil. Eat immediately.

Allow any extra minestrone (without the pasta) to cool completely and store it in the refrigerator for up to 7 days, or in the freezer for several months.

Vegan Minestrone with Miso Pesto

Serves 4 to 6

There is a Provençal vegetable soup, "au pistou," that is something of a French classic—in which a usually mild broth gets livened up at the very end with a dollop of pistou (French pesto) placed onto each bowl. The fresh herbs, garlic, and grated cheese open up in the hot soup, perfuming the bowl and transforming the whole of the meal into something quite lively and comforting.

This recipe is my riff on that classic, making a simple bean and vegetable soup, but blatantly stealing the technique and swapping in vegan Miso-Spinach Pesto (page 117), with the miso taking its comfortable position as a broth enhancer, but emboldened here with nuts and herbs and greens.

In this recipe, I do not recommend a canned bean, as the dried ones will make for a much more flavorful broth (and bean). This also gives a long cook to the vegetables at the beginning, with the bright green crunch of lightly sautéed ones added at the end.

---

2 tablespoons **olive oil**

1 **garlic clove**, chopped

¼ cup diced **white onion**

2 **celery stalks**, diced

1 medium **carrot**, diced

Salt and freshly ground **black pepper**

½ pound **dried beans** (any bean will do, though I have most often used a white bean like cannellini or Great Northern)

1½ cups medium-diced tender **green vegetables** (I like to use zucchini, green beans, and snap peas)

1 cup **Miso-Spinach Pesto** (page 117), or to taste, at room temperature

EQUIPMENT Heavy-bottomed soup pot with a lid or a Dutch oven and a sauté pan or skillet

In a heavy-bottomed soup pot, heat 1 tablespoon of the oil over medium-high heat until shimmering. Add the garlic, onion, celery, and carrot. Season with salt and pepper and sauté until just wilted, about 3 minutes.

Add the dried beans and add water to cover by about 3 inches. Bring to a simmer and season with salt so that the water tastes like it has just barely less salt than a good-tasting broth. Cover the pot and simmer until the beans are fully cooked, keeping an eye on the water level and maintaining at least a half inch of water above the beans. You are looking for cooked beans and a brothy consistency that is not thick like a stew. This can take anywhere from 1 to 3 hours, depending on the beans. When the beans are ready, remove the pot from the heat.

In a sauté pan, heat the remaining 1 tablespoon oil over medium-high heat. Add the green vegetables and season them with salt and pepper. Cook them until they are just barely cooked and still have some bite to them, stirring occasionally, about 2 minutes.

Add the sautéed vegetables to the pot of beans and stir it all together, tasting for seasoning and adjusting as needed (while keeping in mind that the pesto has salt).

Ladle the soup into bowls, topped with a dollop of pesto. Eat immediately, stirring in the pesto as you eat.

Miso Soup

Serves 4

Miso soup is an absolute classic of Japanese cooking, involving miso paste that has been wilted in dashi. Its history dates back, most likely, to the twelfth or thirteenth century, and it is still an incredibly common part of a daily meal. It also happens to be nutritious, low in calories, quite comforting, and very easy to make once you have some dashi lying around. You can use instant dashi powder (available online and in most Japanese markets) in a pinch, or even plain water—though water will make for a far less flavorful soup.

A Japanese breakfast of miso soup, rice, pickles, and a small piece of grilled or broiled fish is, to my mind, a perfect meal.

This is also a highly modifiable soup, with the only truly essential ingredients being the miso paste and liquid. (Small clams, gently simmered in the dashi before the miso is added, are both popular and delicious.)

1 tablespoon **dried wakame**

3½ cups **Vegan Dashi** (page 9)

¼ cup **red miso paste** (or any miso that you have)

¾ cup or so thinly sliced **mushrooms** (button, shiitake, or cremini mushrooms) or whole beech mushrooms

10 ounces **tofu**, ideally silken, drained and cut into bite-size cubes

Salt

1 **scallion**, thinly sliced

Ground **sanshō pepper**, **white pepper**, or **black pepper** (optional)

EQUIPMENT Saucepan or soup pot and a whisk

Place the wakame in a medium bowl and add cold water to cover it by about 1 inch. Let sit to rehydrate.

Meanwhile, in a medium saucepan, heat the dashi over medium heat until warm. Place the miso paste in a medium bowl (or into a large soup ladle) and add 2 to 3 tablespoons of the dashi. Whisk it gently until it is fully combined—this will thin out the miso and keep it from clumping in the soup—then add it to the saucepan a little at a time, whisking constantly.

Bring the soup to a gentle simmer and add the mushrooms and tofu, simmering until the mushrooms are just cooked and the tofu fully warmed, about 2 minutes. Drain the wakame and add it to the pot.

Taste the soup for seasoning and adjust as needed with salt. Ladle it into bowls, topping each with a bit of scallion and a sprinkle of sanshō, white, or black pepper if using.

Shrimp Soupy Rice

Serves 4

This dish pays homage to my stepdad's mother—a Puerto Rican woman from Long Island whose cooking my stepfather raved about. This recipe, developed over many talks with my stepdad, Jimmy, is a riff on his mother's food and the Nuyorican versions of Shrimp Soupy Rice I've had in Manhattan—a soothing, spiced, brothy rice porridge studded with plump bits of shrimp.

If you can find shell-on shrimp, I recommend using those, as you can simmer the shells in the chicken stock for more flavor.

1 pound medium **shrimp**, preferably shell-on

1 tablespoon **tamari**

5 cups **Chicken Stock** (page 5)

5 **garlic cloves**, smashed and peeled

1 small **onion**, roughly chopped

2 **Anaheim chiles** (or any somewhat mild green chile that you can find), seeded and roughly chopped

1 cup roughly chopped fresh **cilantro leaves**, plus more for garnish

1 **celery stalk**, roughly chopped

1 **carrot**, roughly chopped

1 pint **cherry** or **grape tomatoes**

2 tablespoons **olive oil**

1 cup **long-grain white rice**

1 teaspoon **garlic powder**

1 teaspoon **dried oregano**

1 teaspoon **paprika**, preferably smoked

½ teaspoon **ground coriander**

½ teaspoon **ground cumin**

½ teaspoon **ground turmeric**

Salt

Lime wedges, for serving

EQUIPMENT Medium pot, food processor or powerful blender with a tamper (like a Vitamix), Dutch oven or heavy pot with a lid, and a sieve

If the shrimp are shell-on, remove the shells and tails and set aside. Place the shrimp in a medium bowl and add the tamari. Mix and allow it to marinate in the refrigerator until it is needed.

Place the reserved shrimp shells and tails in a medium pot along with the chicken stock, cover, and bring to a bare simmer. Keep warm while you prepare the rest of the ingredients.

In a food processor or blender, combine the garlic, onion, chiles, cilantro, celery, carrot, and tomatoes. Blend them until you have a roughly textured paste—it will probably be quite watery.

In a Dutch oven, heat the olive oil over medium-high heat until shimmering. Add the rice, garlic powder, oregano, paprika, coriander, cumin, and turmeric and stir them frequently, allowing the rice to toast and the spices to become fragrant. Season with salt and allow the rice to toast for an additional 90 seconds or so. Add the blended vegetable mixture and bring to a simmer, then continue simmering it, stirring frequently, until a good amount of the moisture has evaporated, about 4 minutes.

Hold a sieve over the Dutch oven and pour or ladle in the chicken stock, allowing the sieve to catch the shrimp tails and shells. Discard the tails and shells.

Bring everything back to a simmer and then cover and reduce the heat to low. Continue cooking until the rice is just cooked through, about 15 minutes. If the mixture is thickening to the point that it can no longer spread, like a soup, add a little bit of water and return it to a simmer. Taste it for seasoning and add more salt if needed.

Add the shrimp and stir to combine. Cover the pot and let it simmer until the shrimp is just barely cooked through, about 3 minutes longer.

Serve immediately, garnished with cilantro leaves and a wedge of lime.

SEAFOOD SUSTAINABILITY

If you want to try to eat sustainable seafood, but don't know how to gauge what's safe, I have some *really* simple advice for you:

If you only buy seafood sourced in the United States, Norway, and Iceland, you are probably doing the right thing.

How did I come to this conclusion? Well, while working on this book, I asked Peter Kareiva—the president and CEO of the Aquarium of the Pacific, and the former head of the UCLA Institute of the Environment and Sustainability—about an easy, big-picture way to think about seafood sustainability. Basically I asked, "What's something that you can keep in your head that will make seafood sustainability a little easier and more practical?"

He did some research for me, and also contacted Ray Hilborn ("probably the world's leading fisheries biologist"). They looked at a peer-reviewed study from *PNAS* (*Proceedings of the National Academy of Sciences of the United States of America*), studying the top twenty-eight countries in terms of fish production, making up about 80 percent of the global catch. Looking at management and enforcement over the long haul, the top countries were the United States, Norway, and Iceland.

Is this a perfect system? No. But if you keep that information in the back of your head when you shop for seafood, this will get you most of the way there.

Barely Beef Chili

(it's not beef chili)

Serves 6 to 8

Let's just get this out of the way: This is not Texas beef chili. It is not New Mexico Red Chili either, or even that runny and delightful stuff that goes on top of a chili dog. I love all three of those things, albeit in very different ways.

This personal concoction, however, is a healthful stew of red lentils and vegetables with just a bit of ground beef, flavored with lots of garlic, onions, chicken stock, and chili powder. I have often marveled at how red lentils, once cooked down, take on a bit of the texture of stewed ground beef. So I make this as a way to get some of those flavors that I was looking for without having to eat a pile of pure meat. To my mind, this is a much more holistic ratio that I'm happy to eat all week—but it also freezes quite well if you want save some for a cold, tired night in the future. Like most chilis, it is good the first day but tastes even better the next.

Toppings can be personalized, too—with classics like sour cream and cheddar cheese working well, or something lighter like (my favorite version): sliced cilantro, a squeeze of lime, chopped white onion, and a dollop of plain yogurt.

2 tablespoons **olive oil**

1 tablespoon **unsalted butter**

1 cup diced **white onion** (or any onion)

3 **garlic cloves**, finely chopped

1 **serrano chile**, diced (you can substitute any chile you like, removing the seeds and ribs if you want it less spicy)

Salt and freshly ground **black pepper**

1 **zucchini**, diced

1 **yellow squash**, diced

1 bunch **kale** (about 12 leaves), stems and midribs discarded and leaves chopped

1 pound **ground beef** (any fat percentage will be fine)

3 tablespoons **chili powder** (keeping an eye on the ingredient list to see if it includes salt, and if so, using less salt in the rest of your cooking)

1 teaspoon **ground cumin**

In a Dutch oven, heat the oil and butter over medium heat until the butter is melted. Add the onion, garlic, and fresh chile. Season with salt and black pepper and stir it occasionally, until the onion is just wilted, about 3 minutes.

Add the zucchini and yellow squash and season with salt, then stir to combine. Once the pot has returned to a sizzle, add the kale, season with salt, and stir. Once the kale has wilted down a bit, add the ground beef, chili powder, cumin, and garlic powder. Season the beef with salt and black pepper and stir everything together. There is no reason to try to brown your beef in this dish—simply stir it all so that the meat is not cooking in large clumps.

Stir in the red lentils and continue stirring until they are well combined and beginning to sizzle in the pan. Continue cooking, stirring occasionally, until the raw color is cooked out of the beef.

Add the beans and chicken stock and increase the heat to high. Once it is bubbling, reduce it to a gentle simmer, cover, and continue simmering until the lentils are nicely softened, keeping an eye on the amount of liquid and adding water as needed—if the liquid is too thick, the red lentils will take a very long time to cook. This will probably take about 30 minutes.

Once the lentils have softened, add the crushed tomatoes. Return the chili to a gentle simmer, cover, and cook for 1 hour, stirring the bottom of the pot (red lentils sometimes like to stick to the bottom). You should end up with a thick, hearty stew-like consistency. Taste it for seasoning and adjust as needed.

Serve it in bowls with the toppings of your choosing.

1 teaspoon **garlic powder**

1 cup **red lentils**, rinsed

1¾ cups cooked **beans** with their cooking liquid (I prefer red kidney, but any will work), homemade (page 2), or 1 (15-ounce) can beans, undrained

4 cups **Chicken Stock** (page 5)

1 (28-ounce) can **whole peeled tomatoes**, crushed by hand

Topping Options

Diced **white onion**

Sliced **cilantro stems**

Sour cream

Grated **sharp cheddar cheese**

Yogurt

A squeeze of **lime juice**

EQUIPMENT Dutch oven or heavy-bottomed soup pot

Jewish Italian Chicken Noodle Soup

Serves 4 to 6

For the majority of my life, this soup was the only reason I ever made chicken stock. In fact, chicken stock was just a natural by-product on the route to making this. The classic rendition of Jewish deli chicken noodle soup gets vastly improved by the addition of egg noodles cooked separately and kept with some bite left to them, and then the whole thing gets topped with freshly chopped parsley, a lot of black pepper, and most important: a dusting of freshly grated Parmesan cheese. Is it kosher? It is not. But the cheese relaxes into the soup and clings to the shredded chicken and tender egg noodles, making ordinary chicken noodle soup seem clumsy and bland by comparison.

NOTE If you have any leftover chicken, whether from another recipe in this book or even a grocery store rotisserie chicken, this is a lovely way to use some last remaining scraps. But if you don't have that, you can simply buy a chicken breast or two from the store and poach them gently in a pot of water (or even the heated chicken stock) and then leave the chicken to barely simmer until just cooked through. After that, remove the chicken, set aside to cool, and tear it into pieces for soup.

7 cups **Chicken Stock** (page 5)

Salt

8 ounces or so cooked **chicken**, torn by hand (about 1 cup; see Note)

2 medium **carrots**, cut into ½-inch or so rounds (about 1 cup)

3 **celery stalks**, sliced into ½-inch or so pieces (about 2 cups)

1 cup roughly chopped **yellow onion** (from a small to medium onion)

1 (8-ounce) **russet potato**, medium-diced

Noodles and Serving

Salt

12 ounces **extra-wide egg noodles** or **short semolina dried pasta**, such as medium shells or orecchiette

Finely chopped fresh **flat-leaf parsley**

Freshly grated **Parmigiano-Reggiano** cheese

Freshly ground **black pepper**

EQUIPMENT 4-quart or so saucepan or soup pot, a pot large enough to boil noodles, and a colander

In a 4-quart saucepan, bring the chicken stock to a bare simmer over medium heat. Season with salt to taste—it can even be slightly oversalted, as the vegetables and chicken will soak up a lot of that seasoning. Add the chicken, carrots, celery, onion, and potato and return to a simmer. Reduce the heat to a bare simmer, cover, and cook until all of the crunch has left the vegetables but they are not mushy, about 20 minutes. Taste the soup for seasoning and add more salt as needed. Once the vegetables are cooked, you can remove from the heat and keep it covered until you are ready to cook the noodles.

Cook the noodles: When it is time to eat, bring a pot of generously salted pasta water to a boil. Add the egg noodles and cook to al dente according to the package directions. Drain them and portion them into bowls—I like a decent amount of noodles in my bowl, so I tend to fill the bowl about halfway up with noodles. But everyone can do this to their own personal taste.

Ladle the hot soup over the noodles, making sure to get plenty of the broth in. Top the bowls with a sprinkle of parsley, Parmesan cheese, and several hefty cracks of black pepper. Eat right away.

Leftovers reheat quite well—just make sure that you do not, under any circumstances, keep the egg noodles in the pot with the broth. Store leftover noodles and soup separately.

Ginger-Cilantro Chicken Noodle Soup

Serves 4

This is just another way of showing off great stock, by seasoning it with little more than fresh ginger, scallion, and tamari. It is meant to be a brothy, comforting soup that—once you have the chicken stock made—comes together in about 15 minutes. The green vegetables are intended to just barely wilt and remain bright, and the rice noodles make for a perfect accompaniment to soak up the broth and catch the mushrooms and greens on your chopsticks.

NOTE If you have any leftover chicken, whether from another recipe in this book or even a grocery store rotisserie chicken, this is a great way to use some last remaining scraps. But if you don't have that, you can simply buy a chicken breast from the store and poach it gently in a pot of water (or even the heated chicken stock) until just cooked through. After that, you can remove the chicken, set it aside to cool, and then tear it into pieces for soup.

1 (3½-ounce) package **bunashimeji (beech) mushrooms** or 3 ounces or so of other mushrooms, such as white button, cremini, shiitake, or oyster

4 cups **Chicken Stock** (page 5)

3 tablespoons **tamari**

3 **scallions**, thinly sliced, dark green tops kept separate

3-inch knob fresh **ginger**, grated or finely diced (about 2½ tablespoons)

4 ounces **cooked chicken** (see Note), torn into bite-size pieces

6 ounces **rice noodles**, such as mai fun, pad Thai, or vermicelli

Salt

2 small heads **baby bok choy**, very roughly chopped, or about 6 ounces spinach leaves, roughly chopped

Cilantro leaves, for garnish

White sesame seeds, freshly roasted or purchased already toasted

EQUIPMENT Pot large enough to boil noodles and a 4-quart or so saucepan or soup pot

Prepare the mushrooms: For bunashimeji, cut off the dirty root end and discard it, then separate the mushrooms into individual pieces. For cremini or white button, brush off any dirt and thinly slice them. For shiitake or oyster, remove the stems and save them for Vegan Dashi (page 9), then simply tear the caps into bite-size pieces.

Bring a pot of water to a boil for the rice noodles.

Meanwhile, in a 4-quart saucepan, bring the stock and tamari to a gentle simmer. Add the white and light green parts of the scallion, the ginger, chicken, and mushrooms. Bring the broth back to a simmer and then reduce the heat, cover, and keep at a bare simmer for about 10 minutes. Remove from the heat.

Add the noodles to the boiling water and cook according to the package directions. Drain the noodles and divide them among four bowls. Taste the soup for seasoning and add salt if it is needed—it's okay if it is just on the brink of too salty, since there are still noodles and vegetables to go with it.

Add the bok choy or spinach to the pot of soup and stir them in so that they are submerged in broth. Cover the pot again and let the vegetables wilt for about 30 seconds (you want the bok choy stems to be crunchy, or the spinach to keep from going totally limp).

Divide the soup among the bowls, trying to distribute all of the components as evenly as possible. Garnish the bowls with cilantro leaves, the reserved scallion greens, and a light dusting of sesame seeds. Eat right away.

more things in bowls

(rice, and beans, and rice & beans)

← Mushroom and Spinach Bean Bowl with Tamari Butter, Rosemary, and Parmesan, page 142

Krauty Beans

Serves 1 as a main or 2 or 3 as a side

This dish came about because of a somewhat harried need to cook my wife something to eat when I had not been shopping in quite some time. The resulting dish has become such a staple that Iliza now requests I make it on a regular basis. She even cooks it for herself sometimes.

In a way, it is the perfect encapsulation of *Don't Panic Pantry:* a can of beans, a fermented bit of cabbage that can live in the fridge for months on end, some tamari, a clove of garlic, dried oregano, crushed red pepper, and olive oil—all making something deeply nutritious in about 5 minutes, from the staples that you have on hand. It gets weight from the beans, with a tart, probiotic crunch from the sauerkraut, and a hit of umami from the tamari.

1 tablespoon **olive oil**

1 **garlic clove**, roughly chopped

½ cup or so **sauerkraut**, with its juices

1 teaspoon **dried oregano**

¼ teaspoon **crushed red pepper**

1 (15-ounce) can **beans** (any bean is great, but I often use cannellini or pinto), undrained

1 teaspoon **tamari**

Salt

Freshly grated **Parmigiano-Reggiano**, for serving (optional—Iliza usually does, while I usually do not)

Extra-virgin olive oil, for serving

EQUIPMENT Medium skillet

In a medium skillet, heat the oil over medium heat until shimmering. Add the garlic and sauté until it just browned around the edges. Add the sauerkraut and stir, cooking it until it is just beginning to crisp and brown in places and much of the liquid has evaporated, about 2 minutes. Add the oregano, crushed red pepper, and beans and increase the heat to medium-high, stirring the beans frequently. Add the tamari and continue stirring and simmering until the beans have thickened up a bit, and when you drag your spoon across the pan, the beans are slow to fill in the gap, about 2 minutes longer. Season the beans to taste with salt.

Serve in a bowl and top with cheese if you desire, and a drizzle of olive oil.

Quick Beans and Greens for One

Serves 1 (obviously) . . . or 2 if you're both not that hungry

For a great portion of my twenties, I would find myself sitting alone in an apartment, trying to decide what to eat. I would think about all of the quick take-out places near me and usually decide that they were either too expensive or not very good. My general rule of thumb is this: I want everything I eat to either be something that I am extremely excited about, or something that is extremely healthful. Because of this, I would hem and haw for hours on end before ultimately giving up and making this quick bean dish for one. I would then frequently spend any savings by meeting friends at a bar down the street.

These beans are quick (as advertised), nutritious, and extremely inexpensive, comprising little more than beans and greens—in fact, you can even use frozen spinach in a pinch. If you keep these few ingredients on hand, you will always have something that is faster, cheaper, and better for you than mediocre takeout.

If you want some added protein, a runny, fried egg is a great choice, placed right on top.

1 tablespoon **olive oil**

2 **garlic cloves**, smashed with the side of a knife and peeled

4 ounces **soft, leafy greens**, such as spinach, Swiss chard, escarole, or baby kale, roughly chopped (about 4 loosely packed cups), or 1 cup frozen spinach

Salt and freshly ground **black pepper**

1¾ cups **cooked beans**, with their cooking liquid, homemade (page 2), or 1 (15-ounce) can beans (any bean will do, though I have most often used a white bean like cannellini), undrained

Pinch of **dried oregano**

Fried egg (optional)

Squeeze of **lemon juice**, **Charred Tomatillo Salsa** (page 16), or **hot sauce** to finish are optional but quite nice

EQUIPMENT Medium skillet or saucepan

In a medium skillet or saucepan, heat the oil and garlic over medium-high heat and fry it until it is just browned at the edges, about 90 seconds. Add the greens and season them with salt and pepper. Sauté them until they are just wilted, another 90 seconds or so. Add the beans and their liquid, and the oregano. Season again with salt and pepper and reduce to a gentle simmer, stirring the beans until they have thickened up just a bit, about 3 minutes longer.

Transfer the beans and greens to a bowl and top it with a fried egg if you would like. Eat it with the condiment of your choosing. Meeting up with your friends at a bar once you are finished eating is optional, but recommended.

White Beans with Sausage and Kale

Serves 3 or 4

Beans, sausage, and kale form something of a perfect trio—the beans take in the flavorful fat of the sausage, which in turn stews the kale, creating an earthy, hearty, brothy stew that will prepare you for everything from a cold winter night to an evening of heavy drinking, or in some cases both. Think of this, perhaps, as a much easier, faster twist on cassoulet.

This recipe also continues my trend of using meat as a flavoring agent, rather than the primary ingredient in a dinner. Beans flavored with meat, rather than a hunk of meat with a side of greens.

2 tablespoons **olive oil**, plus more for drizzling

4 **garlic cloves**, smashed with the side of a knife and peeled

½ cup diced **shallots** or **onion**

Salt

8 ounces **Cal-Italian Pork Sausage** (page 15) or sweet Italian sausage, casings removed

1 tablespoon **rice vinegar**

12 or so **kale leaves**, stems and midribs stripped and discarded, leaves chopped into bite-size pieces

Pinch of **crushed red pepper**

3½ cups **cooked beans** with their cooking liquid, or 2 (15-ounce) cans beans (any bean will do, though I have most often used a white bean like cannellini), undrained

¼ cup **water**

1 teaspoon **tamari**

Freshly ground **black pepper**

EQUIPMENT Large skillet with a lid or a Dutch oven

In a large skillet, heat the olive oil over medium heat until shimmering. Add the garlic and shallots. Season them lightly with salt and sauté them until they are just wilted, about 90 seconds. Add the sausage and break it up with a spoon. Increase the heat to medium-high, stirring constantly and continuing to break up the sausage with the spoon. Continue cooking until the sausage has started to brown a bit, another 4 minutes or so. Once the sausage has started to crisp, add the rice vinegar, a little at a time, using the spoon and the liquid to deglaze any browned bits from the bottom and edges of the pan.

Once you have deglazed, add the kale and crushed red pepper, season with salt, and continue sautéing and stirring until the kale is wilted and well mixed in, about 3 more minutes.

Add the beans and their juices, the water, tamari, and a few twists of black pepper and stir it all together. Bring it all to a simmer. then reduce the heat to medium-low, cover, and continue simmering for about 5 minutes. Uncover and check: If it has become too thick and starchy, add another splash of water—you want it to have just a little bit of a thick broth to it. Taste it for seasoning, adjusting as needed with salt and black pepper.

Ladle it into bowls and serve it immediately, topped with a drizzle of olive oil.

Mushroom and Spinach Bean Bowl with Tamari Butter, Rosemary, and Parmesan

Makes 2 bowls

This recipe is so much more than the sum of its parts—mushrooms and spinach from the Farmers Market Breakfast (page 27) resting on a bowl of brothy beans, topped off with grated Parmesan, olive oil, and a squeeze of lemon, making for a hearty, vegetarian dinner. While this recipe will work with canned beans, I highly encourage you to try your hand at making A Pot of Beans (page 2), or better yet, a pot of beans with some personalized Bean Variations (page 4), to achieve this decadent, deeply satisfying meal that just so happens to be good for you.

A quick note: If you are one of those people who believes everything is better with a runny egg yolk on it, you will certainly not be disabused of that feeling by adding one here. A poached or sunny-side up egg, its yolk spilling into the broth and coating the beans, is as good a thing here as it is anywhere.

3½ cups **cooked beans** and their cooking liquid, or 2 (15-ounce) cans beans, undrained

2 tablespoons **unsalted butter**

2 sprigs fresh **rosemary**

1½ tablespoons **tamari**

8 ounces roughly torn **mixed mushrooms**, or any mushroom that you like (making sure that you remove any tough stems, like those on shiitakes)

1 tablespoon **olive oil**, plus more for drizzling

3 tablespoons finely chopped **shallots** or **onions**

1 bunch (around 6 ounces) **spinach**, washed and relatively dry

¼ teaspoon **crushed red pepper**

Salt

A poached or sunny-side up **egg**, for serving

½ **lemon**

Parmesan or any sharp aged cheese that you like

EQUIPMENT Covered saucepan, sauté pan, or skillet

If using freshly cooked beans, taste the beans for seasoning and keep them warm. For canned beans or if you are using leftover home-cooked beans, reheat them gently in a covered saucepan on the stove, then taste them for seasoning and keep them warm.

In a sauté pan or skillet, melt the butter over medium heat, then add the rosemary sprigs and allow them to toast for about 30 seconds. Add the tamari and stir to combine, then toss in the mushrooms and sauté, stirring occasionally, until they are fully cooked and tender, about 8 minutes (depending on the types of mushrooms you're using). Discard the rosemary stems, leaving behind any leaves that fell off.

When the mushrooms are just about finished cooking, ladle the hot beans into the bowls. Then once the mushrooms are finished, divide them between the bowls, laying them right on top of the beans. Any extra liquid is encouraged to stay in the sauté pan.

Return the sauté pan to the stove and add the olive oil and shallots and sauté for about 1 minute to just wilt. Increase the heat to high, wait 30 seconds, then add the spinach and the crushed red pepper to the pan. Season lightly with salt and stir constantly until the spinach is just wilted but not mushy, about a minute. Spoon or dump the spinach next to the mushrooms, divided between the two bowls.

If you are using a fried or poached egg, place that atop the bowl now, too.

Squeeze some lemon juice over each bowl (being careful of the seeds). Top with grated cheese and finally a drizzle of olive oil. Eat immediately.

Red Lentil Pomodoro with Spinach and White Beans

Serves 1 or 2

I love the taste of canned tomatoes cooked with garlic and olive oil. It is a soul-satisfying reset for me that I always crave, even when I don't want to eat a bowl of pasta (that's a lie—it's for when I don't think that I *should* eat yet another bowl of pasta). This red lentil dish has become my healthful, fiber-loaded comfort food after an unhealthy work trip, or any time I want some nutritious comfort food—a hearty stew that got me through many nights on my own. Leftovers reheat quite well, too.

Truthfully, you could also call this Lentil Fazool, but I sometimes leave out the beans entirely, making for an even simpler option.

1 tablespoon **olive oil**

3 **garlic cloves**, thinly sliced or chopped

Salt

¼ teaspoon **dried oregano**

¼ teaspoon **dried basil**

Pinch of **crushed red pepper**

6 ounces **spinach leaves** (about 4 cups, tightly packed)

Freshly ground **black pepper**

1¾ cups **cooked beans**, with their cooking liquid, or 1 (15-ounce) can beans (cannellini or any white bean works great), undrained

½ cup **red lentils**, rinsed, cooked until soft, and drained

1 (28-ounce) can **whole peeled tomatoes**

Grated **Parmigiano-Reggiano** cheese, for serving (optional)

Extra-virgin olive oil, for serving

EQUIPMENT Medium pot or saucepan with a lid

In a medium soup pot or saucepan, heat oil over medium heat until shimmering. Add the garlic and a pinch of salt. Stir the garlic and when it has begun to brown around the edges, add the oregano, basil, and crushed red pepper and allow them to toast for 30 seconds. Add the spinach, season with salt and black pepper, and cook until it is just wilted, about 1 minute. Add the beans, along with their juices, season them with salt and black pepper, and stir them until they are simmering and the liquid has thickened up, about 2 minutes.

Add the cooked and drained red lentils and stir them to combine. Allow them to come back up to a simmer. Meanwhile, pour the canned tomatoes and their juices into a bowl and crush them by hand until they have a coarse, rustic texture. Add the tomatoes and their juices to the pot and season again with some salt and pepper.

Bring the pomodoro to a simmer, then cover the pan and reduce the heat to low. Allow it to simmer on low for 5 minutes, then remove it from heat, tasting it for seasoning and adjusting as needed.

Serve the pomodoro ladled into bowls and topped with cheese if you desire (I often do not) and a drizzle of extra-virgin olive oil.

Rice, Warm Greens, and Wilted White Cheddar

Serves 2

This has slowly become one of my favorite dinners in this book—bright, blanched green vegetables tossed with chives and grated garlic that have been quickly bloomed in melted butter, perked up with a squeeze of lemon and laid on a bowl of rice topped with aged white cheddar, which is just barely wilted from the heat of the rice. If you find yourself able to make this dish using spring vegetables from the farmers market, it is highly recommended (though not required).

This dinner came about because my wife and I were in the process of moving out of our home, and I had packed up everything except, it turns out, a strainer, a bowl, a large pot, and a rice cooker. I also happened to have some green vegetables and chive blossoms left over from a farmers market trip a few days earlier, a bit of butter on the counter, and some white cheddar in the fridge.

Any green vegetables will work here (fresh peas, frozen peas, green beans, asparagus, bok choy, broccoli, zucchini, etc.), though I like an assortment—the trick is to cut them all to the same size so that they will cook in around the same time. That being said, if some vegetables are slightly crunchier than others, it just adds to the texture and joy of the dish. If you are a person who demands protein, I would suggest A Perfect Egg (page 12).

This recipe can be halved or doubled with great success.

....

3 tablespoons **unsalted butter**, at room temperature

1 **garlic clove**, finely grated or chopped

1 tablespoon finely chopped fresh **chives**

Salt

4 cups assorted cut **green vegetables**, chopped into ½-inch or so pieces

2 cups or so cooked **rice** (I prefer short-grain Japanese rice), kept hot

1½ ounces **aged white cheddar** or any sharp cheese of your choice, grated into thin ribbons (not preshredded)

1 **lemon**, halved

Freshly ground **black pepper**

1 boiled **egg** (quite optional; page 12)

EQUIPMENT A way to cook rice, a large pot (at least 4-quart) to blanch the vegetables, a large bowl, and a colander

Fill a large pot with water and set it over high heat.

Meanwhile, place the butter in the bottom of a large bowl. If the butter is cold, you can simply microwave it to melt it and then pour it into the bowl, or use the "extra credit" method below. Add the garlic and chives to the butter and set it aside.

Extra credit: If possible, I recommend placing the butter, garlic, and chives in a metal bowl that will fit on top of the pot you are using to boil water for the vegetables. Set the bowl there, like a double boiler, and allow the heat to melt the butter while the water comes to a boil. This will wilt the garlic and chives and infuse the flavor more thoroughly with the butter. Once the water is boiling, you can take off the bowl and set it aside—just be careful because the bowl will be hot.

Once the water is boiling, salt it aggressively—it should be quite briny, like the sea. Add all of the green vegetables and boil them until they have some bite left to them, about 90 seconds (if you are using large, fresh peas, you may want to cook them for an additional 60 seconds or so). Drain them in a colander and immediately (once the water has drained out) dump them in the bowl on top of the butter, garlic, and chives. Leave them there for at least 30 seconds, allowing the residual heat to melt the butter.

Meanwhile, portion the cooked rice into bowls—the wider and flatter the better. Lay the thin ribbons of cheddar over the top of the rice in a single layer.

Squeeze one lemon half over the vegetables (being careful to catch any seeds and discard them). →

← Toss the vegetable mixture thoroughly to combine, making sure to catch all of the butter at the bottom. Taste it for seasoning and add more salt and lemon as needed, as well as a few twists of black pepper.

If you are using a boiled egg, you can slice it in half lengthwise and place a half in the center of each bowl, atop the rice and cheddar.

Lay the vegetables over the rice, surrounding the egg if using, completely covering all of the rice and white cheddar. Eat it immediately.

RICE WASHING

Some people just rinse rice under cold running water in a colander, but I find that to be a little crude and inconsistent. I like to fill a bowl with water, then place the rice in a colander and lower it into the water. Then I use my fingers to gently agitate and swirl the rice so that it is slowly submerged and I can see the water begin to turn cloudy. I will do this for 20 to 30 seconds and then I will lift the rice, dump the water, refill it, and repeat the process.

I typically go with 2 or 3 changes of water. If I'm making short-grain Japanese rice, I often wash it 4 or 5 times, and then allow it to drain and dry in the colander for an hour before cooking (if I have time). It's not essential, but I find that this method helps even mediocre short-grain rice achieve a lovely texture.

Green Rice and Black Beans

Serves 4 to 6

I could very easily eat a plate of rice and beans with a splash of hot sauce several times a week without complaint. A bit of grated cheese, like cheddar, or smoked Gouda, on top is never a bad thing either.

For the rice, I have found myself making a slight riff on classic Mexican arroz verde—a wonderfully fragrant rice turned green from the blending of green chiles, cilantro, and scallions. While chicken stock is often traditional, I find myself only using water and still being quite happy with the outcome. Green rice and beans, with some Charred Tomatillo Salsa (page 16) or hot sauce and a bit of grated cheese is a lovely dinner, made even more complete if you were to add some Sautéed Swiss Chard (page 71) on the side.

For best results, I recommend cooking the rice on the stove, but I have also provided a simpler method using a rice cooker (see Note, below).

Green Rice

3 tablespoons **Ghee** (page 18) or neutral oil, such as vegetable, canola, or grapeseed

1½ cups **long-grain rice**, thoroughly rinsed

4 **scallions**, roughly chopped

1 **garlic clove**, peeled

1 **poblano** or **Anaheim chile**, stemmed and seeded, roughly chopped

1 bunch fresh **cilantro**, leaves and tender stems (parsley can be substituted)

2¼ cups **water**

Salt

Black Beans

1 tablespoon **neutral oil**, such as such as vegetable, canola, or grapeseed

2 tablespoons finely chopped **white onion**

3½ cups cooked **black beans**, homemade (page 2) or from 2 (15-ounce) cans black beans

Salt

For Serving

Charred Tomatillo Salsa (page 16) or hot sauce

Finely grated cheese, such as cheddar, Monterey Jack, or smoked Gouda, for serving

EQUIPMENT Heavy-bottomed pot or a Dutch oven (or you can use a rice cooker) and a medium skillet or sauté pan

Make the green rice: In a heavy-bottomed pot with a lid, such as a Dutch oven, heat the ghee over medium-high heat. Add the rice and toast, stirring it frequently, until it is aromatic and beginning to turn a pale shade of brown, 2 to 3 minutes.

Meanwhile, in a blender, combine the scallions, garlic, chile, cilantro, and water and blend thoroughly.

Once the rice is toasted, add the blender mixture and a healthy pinch of salt to the pot and stir. Bring the mixture to a simmer, then cover the pot, reduce the heat to low, and cook until the liquid is just absorbed, about 12 minutes. Turn off the heat and leave the pot covered for 10 minutes.

Meanwhile, prepare the beans: In a medium skillet or sauté pan, heat the oil over medium-high heat. Add the chopped onion and fry it, stirring occasionally, until it is just wilted but not browning, about 90 seconds. Add the beans and their cooking liquid. Bring them to a simmer and stir frequently until the beans are just slightly thicker, another 90 seconds or so. Remove the beans from heat. Taste and add more salt as needed.

Once the rice has rested, stir it and season it to taste with salt.

Serve the rice and beans together with the salsa or hot sauce of choice and perhaps some grated cheese.

NOTE To make the green rice in a rice cooker, skip the rice toasting step and blend the scallions, garlic, chile, cilantro, and water as directed, but reduce the water to 2 cups. Add the mixture to your rice cooker along with the rice, 2 tablespoons ghee or neutral oil, and a healthy pinch of salt. Give the mixture a stir and then turn on the rice cooker. Once the rice is cooked, fluff up the green rice and season it to taste with salt.

Veggie Scrap Fried Rice

Serves 4 to 6 as a side or 1 as a large meal all to yourself

While carefully prepared fried rice is one of the great foods in the world (shrimp-and-crab is my absolute favorite), fried rice can also stand in as one of the great fridge-clearing dishes of all time. Random bits and scraps of leftover vegetables, the last couple of eggs in the carton, perhaps a knob of leftover steak, a lone raw chicken tender, some diced raw pork shoulder, that quarter of an onion left exposed on a plate that got pushed into the back—they can all go into fried rice.

So while I encourage you to modify and adapt as you wish, I also think that the diced stalks of broccoli and cauliflower are a perfect textural and nutritional complement to a pan of fried rice.

There are a lot of ways to make fried rice—some people like to toast the rice first, others like to simply toss it together with everything (I do both, but most often do more of a toss together at the end, as in this recipe). But one of my favorite tricks (as suggested to me by the photographer Eric Wolfinger, who learned it from chef and cookbook author Charles Phan) is to fry up the egg first—which works as a kind of stabilizing agent that helps to keep the rice from clumping.

NOTE Freshly cooked, short-grain Japanese-style rice, cooked so that the rice is not too gummy, works extremely well. But truthfully, leftover rice is much easier to work with (drier things are almost always easier to fry) and is such a great way to use up leftover cooked rice.

....

2 tablespoons **high-heat oil** (any that you like, such as grapeseed, peanut, or vegetable)

2 large **eggs**, lightly beaten

4 **garlic cloves**, chopped (or any diced alliums you have on hand)

1 tablespoon grated or finely chopped **fresh ginger**

1½ cups assorted **diced veggie scraps**, such as broccoli and cauliflower stalks, frozen peas, corn, carrots, green beans, etc.

Optional **leftover meat scraps**, such as steak, pork, shrimp, or chicken

Salt

2 cups **cooked rice** (either freshly cooked or leftover)

½ tablespoon **tamari** or **soy sauce**

Freshly ground **black pepper**

Splash of **fish sauce** (optional)

Optional Garnishes: **Fish sauce, tamari, rice vinegar, Chile Oil** (page 17) or **sesame oil**, finely chopped **scallions** or **chives**

EQUIPMENT Wok or large nonstick skillet

In a wok or large nonstick skillet, heat the oil over high heat until shimmering. Add the eggs. I like to tilt the egg in the pan and then drag my heatproof silicone spatula or spoon through them to create long, thin strands, and repeat this until they are just barely set. Then use the edge of a spoon or heatproof spatula to break them up into small pieces. Add the garlic, ginger, and assorted veggies (if you are adding some diced bits of meat scraps, they can be added here, too). Season them with a sprinkle of salt and stir frequently until the vegetables are tender and just cooked through, with a touch of bite left to them, 2 to 3 minutes. Mix the ingredients together, continuing to break up the egg and continue stirring. A splash of oil can be added if necessary, but I like to try to avoid it if possible, to keep the rice from getting too greasy. If you are using refrigerated leftover rice, break it up with your fingers so that it is not clumped.

Add the rice and tamari and stir everything thoroughly, allowing it to soak up and combine. Season it to taste with salt and black pepper (I like it a bit peppery) and perhaps a splash of fish sauce if you are so inclined.

Transfer the fried rice to bowls and eat it immediately, seasoning it as you desire with things like fish sauce, rice vinegar, tamari, chile oil, and scallion.

Vegan Mapo Tofu

Serves 2 or 3

Mapo tofu is one of my favorite dishes of all time, originating in the Sichuan province of China—and it has been often imitated, modified, and adapted across the world. Classic Sichuan iterations are usually packed with spicy heat as well as numbing mala spice, and involve ground beef or pork, tofu, chili oil, doubanjiang (a fermented broad bean and chile paste), and douchi (fermented black beans). It is one of the things I am guaranteed to order any time I am at a great Sichuan restaurant.

This version is a lot closer to the popular Japanese iteration—which is far less spicy, with miso paste playing a prominent role in place of the doubanjiang and douchi—but it also takes an idea from my friend Jing Gao, the founder and owner of Fly By Jing, who makes (among other things) their incredibly popular and delicious Sichuan Chili Crisp. Jing uses dried shiitake mushrooms in her mapo tofu in place of meat, and frankly—the meat is not missed.

This recipe doubles quite well if you have a large enough vessel to cook it in.

1 ounce **dried mushrooms,** such as shiitake (see Note)

2 tablespoons **red miso paste** (or whatever miso you have)

4 **scallions**

4 **garlic cloves**, minced

1½ tablespoons **minced fresh ginger**

Salt

¼ cup **Chile Oil** (page 17) or **sesame oil** for less heat

1 teaspoon **shichimi** or ½ teaspoon ground **dried chile de árbol, ichimi,** or **crushed red pepper**

1¾ cups **Vegan Dashi** (page 9); see Note

1 pound **tofu** (ideally silken), cut into ½-inch or so cubes

1 teaspoon **cornstarch** or **potato starch**, dissolved in 1 tablespoon water

Cooked **white rice** (ideally short-grain), for serving

EQUIPMENT Large nonstick skillet or wok

Place the dried mushrooms in a bowl and cover them well with hot water. Allow them to steep until they are fully softened and rehydrated, at least 10 minutes.

In a medium bowl, combine the miso paste with 2 tablespoons of the mushroom soaking liquid and stir it to fully combine (this will help to keep the miso paste from clumping up in the sauce).

Thinly slice the dark green scallion tops and set them aside. Then finely chop the white and light-green parts and add them to the bowl with the miso. Add the garlic and ginger to the bowl.

Drain the rehydrated mushrooms and chop them very finely, then add them to the miso mixture and stir all together to combine. Season the mixture with a sprinkling of salt.

In a large skillet or wok, heat the chile oil over high heat until shimmering. Carefully add the miso mixture and fry it, stirring frequently, until it is fragrant but not burned, about 90 seconds. Add the shichimi and stir it briefly with the miso mixture, then add the dashi, tofu, and cornstarch mixture. Reduce the heat to medium-high and continue simmering the mapo tofu, stirring occasionally, until it has thickened up a bit but is still runny, about 5 minutes. Add half of the green scallion tops and stir them in.

Season the mapo tofu to taste with salt and serve it over cooked white rice, topped with more sliced scallion tops.

NOTE If you'd like, save the leftover rehydrated dried mushrooms used to make the vegan dashi and add to the other mushrooms being soaked, for an extra little punch of umami.

almost entirely proteins

(and some very useful bread crumbs)

← Fillet of Sole, page 159

Herbed Panko Bread Crumbs

Makes about 4 cups

I grew up eating a lot of "Italian Style" bread crumbs that have graced many Italian-American pantries across the country. In my memory, those dusty, dried spice-laden things will always be perfect. But then I was writing a cookbook with Jeremy Fox—a truly brilliant chef who also happens to be my friend—called *On Vegetables*. In it, he made a dish called Daikon Piccata, that used panko bread crumbs (a Japanese variety that is an airier, crispier crumb), pulsed in a food processor with parsley to create a bright-green, ultracrispy bread crumb that I have since gone on to borrow.

Here is my version of Jeremy's bread crumbs—using fresh parsley and garlic to replace the dried versions of my childhood—which I go on to use on traditional dishes I love, dishes like Fillet of Sole (page 159), Mozzarella Marinara (page 157), Chicken Milanesa (page 162), and Chicken Parm (page 165). In a way, these bread crumbs are the perfect encapsulation of the food I grew up eating as a kid, fused with the things I learned in my professional career.

2 **garlic cloves**, roughly chopped

2 cups roughly torn **flat-leaf parsley leaves** (from about 1 bunch parsley)

8 ounces **panko bread crumbs** (ideally without sugar)

Freshly ground **black pepper**

Salt

EQUIPMENT Food processor (see Note)

In a food processor, combine the garlic and parsley and pulse them, occasionally scraping down the sides of the bowl, until you have a finely chopped mixture with no big chunks of garlic left. Add the panko and several twists of black pepper. Pulse the mixture until you have a bright-green, coarse, crumbly bread crumb mixture. Taste it for seasoning and add salt as needed—it should be just on the brink of tasting too salty. Use the herbed bread crumbs immediately, or transfer to an airtight container and freeze them. These bread crumbs freeze very well.

NOTE If you don't have a food processor but still want to make these, chop the parsley and garlic as finely as you possibly can. Then toss them in a large bowl with the panko and salt and pepper to taste, crunching them a bit with your hands as you toss until it is all combined.

Mozzarella Marinara

(that made Iliza cry)

Serves 4

When I was growing up, every Italian restaurant served mozzarella marinara—a thick square of breaded and fried cheese served on a bed of marinara, topped with Parmesan cheese, and eaten with a fork and knife. Somewhere along the line, everything seemed to change, stealing away my childhood and replacing it with mozzarella sticks and marinara dipping sauce. While I understand the reasons for it (stays crunchier longer, etc.), I do not approve of this change. So here is my version, in the way that I always want to eat it.

When I made this on *Don't Panic Pantry,* Iliza took one bite and broke down in tears, live on camera. That moment was a culmination of so much pent-up pandemic frustration and fear, crystallized into crunchy, deep-fried, and sauced cheese, released in a bite of pure pleasure. It is one of my proudest cooking moments.

NOTE If I have the time, I find that breading the mozzarella in advance and leaving it on a wire rack for a few hours in the fridge (or even overnight) yields the best results. But you can also just bread it and fry it right away. The breading may just fall apart a little more.

As for the cheese: Low-moisture mozzarella works best. You can do it with fresh mozzarella, too, but it will tend to run and melt and be a bit soggier. Smoked mozzarella also yields very good results.

8 ounces **low-moisture mozzarella** (ideally in a square log)

½ cup **all-purpose flour,** plus more if needed

2 large **eggs**

¾ cup **Herbed Panko Bread Crumbs** (page 154), plus more if needed

Neutral oil, for pan-frying

About 1¼ cups **Basic Tomato Sauce** (page 94) or **Iliza's Tomato Sauce** (page 96), warmed

Freshly grated **Parmesan cheese,** for serving

A few leaves of chopped fresh **basil** or **parsley** (optional), for garnish

EQUIPMENT Wire rack, sheet pan, and a heavy-bottomed skillet

Slice the mozzarella into 4 square slices of even thickness.

Set up a breading station: Line up three wide plates side by side. Place the flour in the first plate, gently beat the eggs in the second, and place the herbed panko in the third. Set a wire rack into a sheet pan.

Using the wet hand/dry hand method (basically, just keep one hand dry and only touch wet things with the "wet hand"), dredge the first slice of mozzarella in flour so that it is completely coated. Shake off the excess flour and then dip both sides in the egg so that it is coated, too, and let the excess drip off. Finally, dredge it in the herbed panko and set it on the wire rack. Repeat for all 4 pieces, adding more flour, egg, or panko to the plates as needed.

Keep the breaded mozzarella uncovered in the refrigerator until you are ready to fry.

Pour ¼ inch of oil into a heavy-bottomed skillet and place it over medium-high heat. If you have a deep-frying thermometer, you are looking for a temperature of 350°F—but truthfully, I never use one. The basic rule is that you want the cheese to sizzle when it hits the pan, but not to burn. You are looking for steady sizzling sounds. If it does not sizzle, increase the heat, and if it is burning, reduce it. The goal is to achieve a golden brown crust with no blackening or sogginess. →

← Line a plate with a kitchen towel or paper towels and have it near the stove. Begin to lay the first piece into the pan. If it does not sizzle immediately, take it out and wait for the pan to heat further. Cook the mozzarella in batches if necessary—this could mean two, three, or all four at a time, depending on the size of your skillet. Allow it to fry until it is golden brown on the first side, usually 2 to 3 minutes. Then gently flip it over being careful not to splash the oil. If there are spots on the browned side that did not get your desired color, you can spoon the hot oil over it in repeated motions while the other side fries. As each piece becomes golden brown on the second side, remove it and set it on the towel-lined plate. If cooking more batches, just make sure that the oil has returned to the right temperature (the bread crumbs should sizzle when they touch the oil), before you add the next piece of cheese, and add more oil as necessary.

The melted cheese is best if served almost immediately after it has been fried. Ladle some warmed sauce onto a plate and place the mozzarella on top of it. Finish it with grated cheese and a sprinkling of fresh herbs if you so desire. Eat it immediately.

Fillet of Sole

Makes 4 fillets

Fillet of sole was a dinner my brother and I got very excited about. My mom would usually bread it with those previously mentioned Progresso Italian-Style Bread Crumbs, and we would eat it with a squeeze of lemon, a side salad, and a baked potato. I still love this dish, but have modified the breading over the years to use the Herbed Panko Bread Crumbs (page 154). I always used to ask for extra lemons and would absolutely drown my fish in their juice, making it crunchy, salty, soggy, and tart all at the same time.

My mom would always fry it in olive oil—and you can, too—but I find that a neutral oil with a higher smoke point like peanut, grapeseed, or vegetable oil will make your life a little easier. The olive oil is not adding too much flavor, and will scorch and burn much more easily.

We always used sole, but truthfully a thin fillet of any flaky white fish will work—like flounder, tilapia, red snapper, or even catfish. If you can, it is always good to check to see what fish is sustainable (see Seafood Sustainability, page 129). If you are fortunate enough to have a fishmonger or seafood store near you, ask them what they recommend.

NOTE If I have the time, I find that breading the fillets in advance and leaving them on a wire rack for a few hours in the fridge (or even overnight) yields the best results. But you can also just bread them and fry them right away. The breading may just fall apart a little more.

4 skinless **sole fillets** (5 to 6 ounces each)

½ cup **all-purpose flour**, plus more if needed

2 large **eggs**

1 cup **Herbed Panko Bread Crumbs** (page 154), plus more if needed

Neutral oil, for pan-frying

1 **lemon**, quartered, for serving

EQUIPMENT Wire rack, sheet pan, and a heavy-bottomed skillet

Set up a breading station: Line up three plates side by side. Place the flour in the first plate, beat the eggs gently in the second, and place the herbed panko in the third.

Set a wire rack in a sheet pan. Pat the fish fillets dry. Using the wet hand/dry hand method (basically, just keep one hand dry and only touch wet things with the "wet hand"), dredge the first fillet in flour so that it is completely coated. Shake off the excess flour and then dip both sides in the egg so that it is coated, too, and let the excess drip off. Finally, dredge it in the herbed panko and set it on the wire rack. Repeat this with the other fillets, adding more flour, egg, or panko to the plates as needed.

Keep the fillets uncovered in the refrigerator until you are ready to fry.

Line a plate with a kitchen towel or paper towels and have it near the stove. Pour ¼ inch oil into a heavy-bottomed skillet and place it over medium-high heat. If you have a deep-frying thermometer, you are looking for a temperature of 350°F—but truthfully, I never use one. The basic rule is that you want the fillets to sizzle when they hit the pan but not burn. You are looking for steady sizzling sounds. If they do not sizzle, increase the heat, and if they are burning, reduce it. The goal is to achieve a golden brown crust with no blackening or sogginess.

Lay your first fillet in the pan. If it does not sizzle immediately, take it out and wait for the pan to heat further. Cook the fillets in batches—this could mean one or two at a time, depending on the size of your skillet. Allow it to fry until it is golden brown on the first side, usually 2 to 3 minutes. →

← Then gently flip it over being careful not to splash the oil. If there are spots on the browned side that did not get your desired color, you can spoon the hot oil over it in repeated motions while the other side fries. Once the fillet turns golden brown and the fish is cooked through, set the fillet on the towel-lined plate. You are looking for an internal temperature of about 145°F, but if the fillet is not too thick, your fish will be cooked by the time both sides are golden brown.

Repeat for the remaining fillets, making sure that your oil is back at the right temperature (the bread crumbs should sizzle when they touch the oil) before you add the next fish and adding more oil as necessary.

Once they are cooked, serve them immediately with lemons for squeezing.

Chicken Milanesa

Makes 4 chicken cutlets

This is quite similar to the Fillet of Sole (page 159), with the added bonus that I am much more interested in eating these cold leftovers out of the fridge the next day than I am fish. It also has the benefit of being able to be turned into Chicken Parm (page 165).

I find that a neutral oil with a higher smoke point like canola, grapeseed, or vegetable oil will make your life a little easier. The olive oil is not adding too much flavor, and will scorch and burn much more easily.

NOTE If I have the time, I find that breading the chicken in advance and leaving it on a wire rack for a few hours in the fridge (or even overnight) yields the best results. But you can also just bread it and fry it right away. The breading may just fall apart a little more.

4 boneless, **skinless chicken breasts** (you can use boneless, skinless thighs, too, but I find the breasts are preferable for this dish)

¾ cup **all-purpose flour**, plus more if needed

2 large **eggs**, plus another if needed

1¼ cups **Herbed Panko Bread Crumbs** (page 154), plus more if needed

Neutral oil, for pan-frying

1 **lemon**, quartered, for serving

EQUIPMENT Plastic wrap or a large zip-seal plastic bag, wire rack, sheet pan, and a heavy-bottomed skillet

Pat the chicken breasts dry and then set one on your cutting board. The goal here is to take the rounded breast of uneven thickness and turn it into something that is fairly uniform in thickness (this will make for even cooking and frying). Lay your hand flat against the top of the breast and then hold your sharp kitchen knife parallel to it and the cutting board. You are looking to slide your knife into the center of the thickest part, and then glide it back toward the other side, stopping about ½ inch from the other edge. Then you can pull out your knife and open the chicken breast like a book. It should now be one big, thin, wide chicken breast. Repeat this process with the other breasts.

Next, to really make it even, lay a breast between two sheets of plastic wrap or inside a large zip-seal bag. Use a meat mallet, wine bottle, or rolling pin to pound the meat (without too much force) until it is of even more uniform thickness. Once you are done, set the breast aside and repeat it with the others.

Set up a breading station: Line up three wide plates side by side. Place the flour in the first plate, gently beat the eggs in the second, and place the herbed panko in the third.

Set a wire rack inside a sheet pan. Using the wet hand/dry hand method (basically, just keep one hand dry and only touch wet things with the "wet hand"), dredge the first piece of chicken in the flour so that it is completely coated. Shake off the excess flour and then dip both sides in the egg so that it is coated, too, and let the excess drip off. Finally, dredge it in the herbed panko and set it on the wire rack. Repeat this with the other pieces, adding more flour, egg, or panko to the plates as needed.

Keep the breaded cutlets uncovered in the refrigerator until you are ready to fry.

Line a plate with a kitchen towel or paper towels and have it near the stove. Pour ¼ inch oil into a heavy-bottomed skillet and place it over medium-high heat. If you have a deep-frying thermometer, you are looking for a temperature of 350°F—but truthfully, I never use one. The basic rule is that you want the chicken to sizzle when it hits the pan but not burn. You are looking for steady sizzling sounds. If it does not sizzle, increase the heat, and if is burning, reduce it. The goal is to achieve a golden brown crust with no blackening or sogginess.

Lay one of the chicken cutlets in the pan. If it does not sizzle immediately, take it out and wait for the pan to heat further. Cook the chicken in batches—this could mean one or two at a time, depending on the size of your skillet. Allow it to fry until it is golden brown on the first side, about 4 minutes. Then gently flip it over being careful not to splash the oil. If there are spots on the browned side that did not get your desired color, you can spoon the hot oil over it in repeated motions while the other side fries. Once the cutlet is golden brown and the chicken is cooked through, remove the piece and set it on the towel-lined plate. You are looking for an internal temperature of about 150°F, but chicken pounded into a thinnish cutlet is usually cooked by the time that both sides are golden brown.

Repeat this with the other pieces, making sure that your oil is back at the right temperature (the bread crumbs should sizzle when they touch the oil) before you add the next piece of chicken and adding more oil as necessary.

Once they are cooked, serve them immediately with lemons for squeezing.

Chicken Parm

Serves 4

If you happen to be making Chicken Milanesa (page 162) and you want to make it a little more decadent, this is a great way to go about doing it. It is a simple process, that merely requires slicing mozzarella and placing it on top of the chicken, then melting and partially browning it under a broiler. While it may well be carbohydrate overkill, I often serve it with a side of pasta tossed with tomato sauce. While I would choose something like rigatoni or fusilli, Iliza does not understand how anyone could want this with anything other than capellini.

Chicken Milanesa (page 162)

2 cups **Basic Tomato Sauce** (page 94) or **Iliza's Tomato Sauce** (page 96), warmed, plus 1½ cups to serve with the pasta

8 ounces **mozzarella cheese** (fresh or low-moisture are both fine), thinly sliced

Freshly grated **Parmesan** cheese

Fresh **basil leaves** (optional)

8 ounces dried **pasta** (your choice of shape), cooked

EQUIPMENT Sheet pan and a wire rack

Preheat the broiler (or if you don't have a broiler, set your oven to the highest heat possible; you may not be able to achieve any browning on your cheese, but it will melt). Line a sheet pan with foil. If you have a wire rack, set it in the pan. It will be a little easier to manage if you have the wire rack, but it is not essential.

Place the chicken pieces on the wire rack or directly on the lined baking sheet. Top each chicken breast with a spoonful of the tomato sauce, then lay the mozzarella slices on top of the chicken and top it all with some grated Parmesan. Transfer to the oven and cook until the cheese is melted and browned to your liking, keeping an eye on the chicken so that it does not burn. If the edges begin to burn, remove the chicken and serve it (burned chicken is bad, no matter how brown your cheese gets).

Serve immediately, plated atop a few spoonfuls of warmed tomato sauce, and a side of your preferred pasta with your preferred tomato sauce.

Turkey Meatballs

Makes 10 to 12 meatballs

While I enjoy a classic, crumbly Italian-American meatball with beef, pork, and veal, these are the meatballs that I would eat as a main course all on their own. They are loaded with craggy, rustic hunks of fresh herbs and onion and garlic, and since turkey is especially lean, they include rather a lot of Parmesan cheese to add both fat and flavor. I like to make these with either fresh basil or parsley—whichever I have on hand.

I usually eat it with some blanched broccoli or a light salad and maybe a side of pasta if I'm so inclined. But they can also be simmered in either of the basic tomato sauces in this book and turned into Spaghetti and Turkey Meatballs.

This recipe, to my surprise, works well with white or dark meat (I always used a mixture, but Iliza always wants just the breast). The dark meat just requires more cooking.

I tend to make these meatballs fried in a pan, but they can also be roasted in the oven, with excellent results. Some people prefer the oven for an easier cleanup, while other people don't want to fire up a whole oven just to cook meatballs. Both methods work really well, so I include them for you here.

1 pound **ground turkey**

⅓ cup or so **panko bread crumbs** or **plain dried bread crumbs**

2 **garlic cloves**, grated or minced

3 tablespoons diced **onion** or **shallot**

About ½ ounce **Parmigiano-Reggiano** cheese, grated (about ½ cup if grated on a fine Microplane; or ¼ cup on a conventional grater)

3 tablespoons finely chopped fresh **parsley** or ½ cup fresh **basil leaves**, roughly torn

¼ teaspoon **dried oregano**

Pinch of **crushed red pepper**

¼ teaspoon freshly ground **black pepper**

1 large **egg**

Salt

Neutral oil, such as grapeseed, vegetable, or canola (or if you are my mom, olive oil)

EQUIPMENT Heavy skillet, muffin tin or sheet pan, and a meat thermometer

Place the ground turkey in a large bowl. Add almost all of the bread crumbs to the bowl (you will adjust this later, based on the feel of the mixture). Add the garlic, onion, Parmesan, fresh herbs, dried oregano, crushed red pepper, black pepper, and egg. Add a healthy pinch of salt and then fold the mixture together, making sure to keep it all light and airy—fully combining all of the ingredients without compacting it and making it dense. You want to have a light touch, but also make sure that it is thoroughly mixed.

This will be a somewhat wet, tacky mixture, but if it feels at all slick and won't hold shape, fold in a little bit more bread crumbs.

WAIT! Do a Test Run Before Cooking All the Meatballs Place a heavy skillet over medium-high heat and add just a drizzle of oil. Pinch off about a ½-inch ball of the meat mixture and squish it down into a loose patty. Once the oil is hot, lay the patty in the oil and let it fry until golden brown, then flip it over and brown the other side. Once both sides are browned, turn off the heat and remove the patty, allowing it to cool briefly. Taste it for seasoning. If it needs more salt or pepper, add more to the turkey mixture and fold it in. If the patty fell apart in the pan, you may want to add a teaspoon or so more bread crumbs.

Cover the meatball mixture and keep it refrigerated until you are ready to cook it. (I find that they are better when they've had a chance to sit for at least 30 minutes, but you can also cook them right away, or store them in the refrigerator for a day.)

When it's time to cook, use gentle hands to shape the meatballs: Take a gob of the mixture and roll it between your palms—you are looking for a meatball that is about 2 inches wide, or just larger than a golf ball. They should feel loose but also able to hold their shape. Don't be concerned if there are large hunks of herbs spilling out—I find them quite beautiful. →

← Pan-Fry Method Heat the skillet over medium-high heat and add enough oil to coat the bottom of the pan quite comfortably. You will know the oil is hot enough if you place in a meatball and it sizzles immediately. Working in batches if necessary (to avoid overcrowding the pan), place your meatballs in the pan with some space around each one. If the meatballs begin to blacken at all, reduce the heat. If they are not sizzling, increase the heat. If the oil level gets too low, simply add a little more and keep an eye on the temperature.

Once a meatball has turned golden brown, use tongs to turn it onto another side. Continue turning the meatballs as needed, or shaking the pan to roll them if you are so inclined. You may find that your meatballs flatten a bit as they fry, and turn more into thick, triangular wedges—fortunately, the odd shapes will taste just as good as perfect spheres.

Continue cooking until they are cooked through and, ideally, golden brown. The center of the meatballs should register at 150°F for breast meat, or 165°F for dark meat (see Note).

Once each meatball is done, remove it from the pan and place it on a wire rack or a plate lined with paper towels. Let them cool briefly before eating.

Oven Method Preheat the oven to 450°F. Lightly grease a muffin tin or line a sheet pan with parchment.

Arrange the meatballs either into individual muffin cups or spaced out evenly on the sheet pan. Roast the meatballs for 7 minutes. Turn them over to brown the other side and continue roasting until they register at 150°F for breast meat or 165°F for dark meat (see Note), 5 to 10 minutes longer.

Let the meatballs cool briefly before serving.

NOTE If you plan to eat the meatballs in tomato sauce, you don't have to worry about the internal temperature yet. Instead, simply get them browned to your liking and then transfer them to a pot of simmering tomato sauce to finish cooking. Let them simmer away until it's time to serve them up.

NOTE 2 For what it's worth, the USDA has one doneness temperature for all ground poultry, regardless. It's 165°F.

Sheet-Pan Miso Roast Chicken with Vegetables

Serves 3 or 4

My mom used to roast a trussed chicken on a bed of onions, surrounded by root vegetables, and I always loved the feeling of an entire dinner for three—my mother, my brother, and me—all cooked in one pan. I wanted to make my own version, using the deep, umami flavor of red miso paste to amp things up. I tried several different versions before finally finding one that I was happy with. As it happens, Iliza and I actually enjoyed the ritual of roasting a chicken every week, each time with slight tweaks, until we found the right one.

There is a little bit of prep involved in this, but what I love the most about it is that you can get all of that work done in the morning, or even the night before, and keep it all in the fridge. Then when you are ready to eat, you just have to take it out of the fridge and put it in the oven, roast it, and eat it.

As with the other roast chicken in this book, I highly encourage you to find a smaller chicken if you can—though this can often be difficult. I find that chickens in the 3- to 3½-pound range tend to be more flavorful and cook more easily—though most grocery store chickens tend to be closer to 4, 5, or even 6 pounds.

....

½ cup **red miso paste** (or any miso will do)

3 tablespoons **olive oil**

1 tablespoon **tamari**

1 tablespoon **red wine vinegar**

2 **garlic cloves**, grated

1 teaspoon grated fresh **ginger**

1 whole **chicken** (ideally under 4 pounds)

1 large **sweet potato** (about 12 ounces), cut into ½-inch pieces

1 small **onion**, roughly chopped

12 ounces **cauliflower florets**, broken into bite-size pieces

Salt

EQUIPMENT Poultry shears (optional), sheet pan, meat thermometer

In a large bowl combine the miso, 2 tablespoons of the olive oil, the tamari, vinegar, garlic, and ginger and whisk them together until you have a combined paste.

Pat the chicken dry with a towel and then spatchcock it: Poultry shears make for the easiest method, but you can also do it with a good sharp knife. Set the chicken breast-side down on a cutting board. Locate the backbone and use shears or your knife to cut along both sides of the backbone by simply cutting through the flesh just next to the hard edge of the backbone. Remove the backbone and save it for things like Chicken Stock (page 5). Flip the chicken back over and lay it so that its legs are laid flat and the breast is facing up. Press down on the breast with the heel of your palm—you should hear a little crack in the bones, allowing the chicken to lie flat on the board.

Scoop out about half of the miso mixture and slather it over the outside of the chicken, going heavier on the breasts and legs than the back, making sure to get all of the crevices between the legs and breast. Line a sheet pan with foil and lay the chicken breast-side-up on the pan. Tuck the wings back to prevent them from burning.

Add the chopped vegetables to the bowl with the rest of the miso mixture. Add the remaining 1 tablespoon oil and season the mixture lightly with salt. Toss it thoroughly to combine. Scatter the vegetables in an even layer on the sheet pan, around the chicken.

If you are salt-averse, leave the chicken as is. If you like things a little bit saltier, a light sprinkle of salt is good, too. You can roast the chicken right away, or you can leave it uncovered in the refrigerator for up to 36 hours or so.

When you are ready to cook, position a rack in the center of the oven and preheat the oven to 425°F. →

← Transfer the sheet pan to the oven and roast until a meat thermometer inserted into the thickest part of the breast registers 150°F, and the thickest part of the thigh registers 165°F. If you find that the chicken is beginning to burn but the inside is not cooked, you can cover it with a sheet of foil for a bit. Just remember to remove it again for the last few minutes to prevent trapped steam from making the skin especially soggy. The cook time can vary greatly depending on the size of the chicken, but 45 minutes is a good rough gauge.

Allow the chicken to rest for at least 10 minutes. Carve it into pieces, or eat it with your hands while standing over the stove, as Iliza and I tend to.

Crispy Roast Chicken with Chile-Scallion Butter

Makes 1 chicken, serving 2 to 4 people

Crispy-skinned chicken is very hard to achieve in the oven. It is a battle against moisture in its many forms, frequently taking a skin that was crispy right after it was roasted, and then gradually turning it soft the longer it sits. Unfortunately, you have to rest a chicken after it roasts, or else even a perfectly cooked one will leak its juices and get dry and rubbery.

This chicken attempts to remain crispy through a few tricks: spatchcocking (or butterflying) the chicken helps to make a chicken that will allow the thighs and breasts to finish cooking at the same time, while doing so at a higher heat that lends itself better to crisping. Salting the chicken and letting it air-dry overnight in the fridge helps a lot, too—it is essentially a dry brine that concentrates the flavor and removes excess moisture (moisture, again, is the enemy of crispy skin). A final sprinkling of baking powder is a great trick, too, which bubbles and puffs and expands the skin, creating a thinner, wider surface, lending itself to even more crispiness.

Rather than simply shoving butter under the skin, I love to make a compound butter of dried chile de árbol and scallions—turning this humble chicken into the spicy, crispy, roasted chicken of your dreams. Some of that butter will get turned into a tart, spicy lemon butter sauce, meant to accompany the breast meat (which will never be as flavorful or delicious as the thighs, wings and drumsticks).

If you are in a hurry, you can skip the overnight process (see Note), and it will still be quite delicious. As for the chicken itself, try to find one closer to 3½ pounds. This will result in a better tasting, more evenly cooked chicken, while also allowing the flavors of the butter compound to penetrate more thoroughly.

This chicken pairs quite well with a side of Krauty Beans (page 138) or even just some boiled rice and steamed broccoli.

1 whole **chicken** (ideally under 4 pounds)

Kosher salt

7 **chiles de árbol** or any small dried red chiles you like, stemmed, or 1 tablespoon **crushed red pepper**

4 **scallions**, roughly chopped

3 **garlic cloves**, roughly chopped

1 stick (4 ounces) **unsalted butter**, at room temperature

¼ teaspoon **baking powder**

¼ cup fresh **lemon juice**

5 tablespoons **water**

EQUIPMENT Poultry shears (optional), sheet pan, wire rack, food processor (or a willingness to very finely chop things by hand), and a meat thermometer

Pat the chicken dry with a towel and then spatchcock it: Poultry shears make for the easiest method, but you can also do it with a good sharp knife. Set the chicken breast-side down on a cutting board. Locate the backbone and use shears or your knife to cut along both sides of the backbone by simply cutting through the flesh just next to the hard edge of the backbone. Remove the backbone and save it for things like Chicken Stock (page 5). Flip the chicken back over and lay it so that its legs are laid flat and the breast is facing up. Press down on the breast with the heel of your palm—you should hear a little crack in the bones, allowing the chicken to lay flat on the board. (If you are roasting the chicken on the same day, read the Note at the end of the recipe. If you are dry-brining the chicken overnight, continue to the next step.)

Line a sheet pan with foil and set a wire rack on top.

Season the chicken with what will seem like far too much salt—you almost cannot add too much. This will dry out the chicken overnight, and you will brush off any excess salt later, leaving it perfectly brined.

Once the whole of the chicken is thoroughly salted, lay it on the rack, breast-side up, and leave it uncovered in the fridge for at least 6 hours and up to 36 hours.

Meanwhile, make the chile-scallion butter. You can do this ahead of time and refrigerate it, or make it shortly before you plan on roasting the chicken. In a food processor, combine the chiles, scallions, and garlic and pulse them until you have something of a paste, scraping down the sides of the bowl as needed (or chop them very, very finely by hand). Add the butter and blend it all together, scraping down the sides as needed, until you have a unified compound butter. Measure out 4 tablespoons of the compound butter and put it in the fridge (this will be for the butter sauce). Transfer the remaining butter to a container and keep it covered at room temperature for up to 4 hours. If making ahead and refrigerating, just be sure to let it come back to room temperature before using.

When ready to roast, preheat the oven to 450°F.

Brush off any excess salt from the chicken. Separate the skin from the chicken with your hands—it can be a somewhat gruesome sounding task, but quite worth the effort—by gently moving your fingers underneath the skin of the chicken, both on the breast and legs. Separate the membrane, creating a loose skin without tearing it, if possible. This will make for a crispier skin, while also giving you a place to add the compound butter.

Once separated, use a spoon (or your hands) to spread the room-temperature compound butter underneath the skin of the chicken, trying to distribute it as thoroughly as possible under the skin of the breasts, thighs, and drumsticks. Use any excess butter on your hands or in the bowl to rub the wings and then tuck them back behind the chicken. Finally, sprinkle the outside of the chicken with the baking powder.

Place the chicken back on the wire rack, breast-side-up and transfer to the oven. Roast until a meat thermometer inserted into the thickest part of the breast registers 150°F and the thickest part of the thigh registers 165°F. The cook time can vary greatly, but 45 minutes is a good rough gauge.

Let the chicken rest for at least 10 minutes before carving and serving.

Meanwhile, to make the butter sauce, in a saucepan, combine the lemon juice and water and bring it to a boil over medium-high heat. Take the 4 tablespoons reserved cold compound butter from the fridge and divide it into four chunks. Once the liquid has reduced by half, reduce the heat to medium, add the first piece of butter and whisk it constantly to incorporate it. Once it is dissolved, add the next one. Continue repeating until you have a unified sauce. If the sauce has separated you can add a few drops of water and whisk it again to help bring it back together. Season it to taste with salt and serve it on the side with the chicken.

NOTE If you won't be dry-brining the chicken overnight and plan on roasting the same day, after spatchcocking the chicken, set it breast-side up on a wire rack in a foil-lined sheet pan. Make the chile-scallion butter as directed and smear under and over the skin. Sprinkle the chicken with a generous seasoning of kosher salt around the whole of the outside of the chicken, then follow it with the baking powder. The rest of the recipe is the same.

ACKNOWLEDGMENTS

Her recipes already grace so many of these pages, but I want to take another moment to say thank you to my mom, Nancy, who instilled the importance of knowing how to cook into all of her children. She taught us that cooking is not just a hobby—it is a mandatory life skill.

To my dad, Albhy, an outstanding breakfast cook, whose matzoh brie (heavy on matzoh, light on brie) will always be the gold standard: thank you for being a compassionate, loving dad.

Thank you to Melanie, my stepmother, for loving my brother and me, and for laughing when you found out that I tried to clean a microwaved enchilada spill on our carpet by using bleach. Thank you to Jimmy, my stepdad, for always being there for us, at literally any hour. Thank you, Gabriela, for your unrelenting kindness; and Jacob for both your academic and literal appetite.

To Jason (Shantam), my older brother: thank you for all the lessons you learned and suffered for instead of me; and for handing over your chai and kitchari recipes for this book. As a result, I forgive you for throwing rocks at me.

Thank you, Peter Kareiva, for your tremendous efforts guiding my education—and the writing in this book—on sustainability, nutrition, and their complicated relationship with each other.

Thank you to my agent, Alison Fargis, who invested countless hours of tough editing and encouragement in me, long before we ever earned a dollar together, and who has been on the receiving end of a slew of both frustrated and overly excited emails. Thank you for telling me when to turn money down. Thank you for believing in me.

To Lexy Bloom: I think back often to the time I met with you in your office in New York and we talked for quite a while about life and cookbooks and you asked me, "If you could write any cookbook, what would it be?" I told you what it would be, with the caveat that I knew that I wasn't a big enough deal to get my own cookbook. You said, "Not necessarily," and told me to write a proposal. I wrote it that winter, on vacation in Vermont. After some world-shifting twists and turns, that became this book. There is no one in the world I would rather have written it with.

I would also love to thank the truly exceptional team at Knopf: Reagan Arthur (I'm so glad you liked the Rosemary-Tamari Almonds!), Kathy Hourigan, Andy Hughes, Anna Knighton (the colors!), Jenny Carrow, Nicole Pedersen, Lorraine Hyland, Sarah New, Morgan Fenton, and Morgan Hamilton. You all, genuinely, made my dream come true.

To Kristin Teig: thank you for your truly outstanding photography in this book. You brought incredible energy and brilliant, thoughtful ideas every single day, resulting in a far more beautiful book than I had ever envisioned. Let's please work together again, as soon as humanly possible.

Thank you Carrie Ann Purcell, for your elegant and seemingly effortless food styling. Over the course of this cookbook shoot you became, perhaps, the only person I've ever truly trusted to cook in my home. Please help me prepare Thanksgiving dinner next year.

To David K. Peng, our maestro of props and photography assistant: your enthusiasm, attitude, and outstanding eye (I want all of those plates and bowls in my home now) brought life to our shoot. Thank you for helping to build a beautiful book and a wonderful work environment.

Thank you, James Starr, for being the kind of person who, countless times, created a job that fit my particular brain, versus shoving me into places I did not belong.

To Kevin Bludso: thank you for putting me in charge of a restaurant that carried your name, for the life lessons and cooking lessons, and for many nights drinking brown spirits and talking shit (with many more to come).

Jeremy Fox: thank you for giving me my first chance to write a cookbook, for teaching me about food and cooking in a way that literally no one else in the world could. (Insert: very-dry Jeremy joke about something I didn't thank him for.) Thank you, Rachael Sheridan, for convincing him to write the book at all, let alone with me.

Last but certainly not least: thank you to the Kick-Its, the Ham Swirls, and all of the fans of *Don't Panic Pantry,* for gathering together during a frightening pandemic to cook and laugh with us. You probably kept me from going insane.

A NOTE ON SOURCES

Here is a list of the most important published articles and studies I read in researching this book. These were heavily referenced for any writing in this book on nutrition and sustainability. These were mostly vetted and discovered via the incomparable Peter Kareiva.

Alpert, Patricia T. "Sugar: The Good, the Bad, and the Ugly Facts." *Home Health Care Management & Practice* 24, no. 4 (2012): 208–210.

Kumar, Chandini Shantha, Amanat Ali, and Annamalai Manickavasagan. "Health Benefits of Substituting Added Sugars with Fruits in Developing Value-Added Food Products: A Review." *International Journal of Nutrition, Pharmacology, Neurological Diseases* 10, no. 3 (2020): 75–90.

Martínez Steele, Eurídice, Larissa Galastri Baraldi, Maria Laura de Costa Louzada, Jean-Claude Moubarac, Dariush Mozaffaraian, and Carlos Augusto Monteiro. "Ultra-Processed Foods and Added Sugars in the US Diet: Evidence from a Nationally Representative Cross-Sectional Study." *BMJ Open* 6, no. 3 (2016).

Melnychuk, Michael C., Emily Peterson, Matthew Elliott, and Ray Hilborn. "Fisheries Management Impacts on Target Species Status." *Proceedings of the National Academy of Sciences* 114, no. 1 (December 2016): 178–183.

Monteiro, Carlos A. "Nutrition and Health. The Issue Is Not Food, nor Nutrients, So Much as Processing." *Public Health Nutrition* 12, no. 7 (2009), 729–731.

Poe, Kristen L. "The Detrimental Health Effects of Sugar." *Journal of Obesity and Diabetes* 1, no.1 (2018): 21–22.

Qi, Xin, and Richard Tester. "Is Sugar Extracted from Plants Less Healthy Than Sugar Consumed Within Plant Tissues? The Sugar Anomaly." *Journal of the Science of Food and Agriculture* 101, no. 6 (April 2021): 2194–2200.

Reynolds, Andrew, Jim Mann, John Cummings, Nicola Winter, Evelyn Mete, and Lisa Te Morenga. "Carbohydrate Quality and Human Health: A Series of Systematic Reviews and Meta-Analyses." *The Lancet* 393, no. 10170 (January 2019), 434–435.

Yang, Quanhe, Zefeng Zhang, and Edward W. Gregg. "Added Sugar Intake and Cardiovascular Disease Mortality Among US Adults." *JAMA Internal Medicine* 174, no. 4 (2014): 516–524.

SEE, WE TOLD YOU IT WAS MOSTLY VEGETARIAN

(but also often vegan and gluten-free)

Vegan (or "still very good and vegan if you omit the cheese")

Gluten-Free

INDEX

(Page references in *italics* refer to illustrations.)

a note about the author

Noah Galuten is a chef, James Beard Award–nominated cookbook author, and host of the YouTube cooking show *Don't Panic Pantry*. He currently lives in Los Angeles with his wife, daughter, and small dog.

a note on the type

The text of this book was set in Plantin, a typeface first cut in 1913 by the Monotype Corporation of London. Though the face bears the name of the great Christopher Plantin (ca. 1520–1589), who in the latter part of the sixteenth century owned, in Antwerp, the largest printing and publishing firm in Europe, it is a rather free adaptation of designs by Claude Garamond made for that firm. With its strong, simple lines, Plantin is a no-nonsense face of exceptional legibility.

Composed by North Market Street Graphics, Lancaster, Pennsylvania
Printed and bound by C&C Offset, China
Designed by Anna B. Knighton